A Peaceful Pathway for Separating Couples

KIRSTY SALVESTRO

A huge thank you to:

All of my lovely clients who have trusted me enough to allow me to support and guide you on your journey. Thank you.

To my kind and caring colleagues who make this work possible. You are so important and so essential in this world.

To each and every member of my writing group and our fearless leader Andrew Griffiths, for being so inspirational and kind along the way.

To Michael, Anna and the rest of the team at Publish Central. Your work is amazing and so appreciated. You have made this really happen.

To my family and friends, especially my beautiful book buddy, thank you for your everlasting love and support.

Finally, but most importantly, to my amazing husband and beautiful children, I could never have done this without you. Your faith in me is what kept me going. You are the reason I wrote this book. I want the world to be a better place for you to live in.

To all the separating couples out there who
are looking for a better, kinder and calmer pathway.
It is time to start making good choices following separation;
education and knowledge are the key.
Choose to stop fighting. Choose your family.
Choose you.

First published in 2021 by Kirsty Salvestro

A catalogue entry for this book is available from the National Library of Australia.

ISBN: 978-1-922391-64-3

Printed in Australia by McPherson's Printing
Project management and text design by Publish Central
Cover design by Peter Reardon

The paper this book is printed on is certified as environmentally friendly.

Contents

Introduction

A declaration of peace

'To fight and conquer in all our battles is not supreme excellence; supreme excellence consists of breaking the enemy's resistance without fighting.'

Sun Tzu

Two years ago, I came to the personal decision that I did not want to fight anymore. I was tired, it made me unhappy and I was not enjoying my work. As a family lawyer, I felt like I had to fight every day, despite the fact that this was not in my nature. At the same time, I came to the realisation that if I led the way for couples and showed them how *not* to fight, then not only would my world be different, so would theirs.

So, I stopped fighting.

You can too.

A simple declaration of peace is required if humans want to survive and live in peace and harmony. The one thing I know for certain is that peace is so much greater than the alternative. The fighting, cruelty, hatred. The war. History has taught us that war results in devastation and destruction.

Sadly, during my time as a family lawyer, I've seen far too many people choosing war over peace. Knowing this is not necessary, it's my mission to change the frequency with which this occurs.

Why do so many people choose war over peace?

Following a separation, peace, kindness and happiness are what people hope for and what we truly need to flourish. Why then do so many turn to the alternative, the unpleasantness, the sadness and the bitterness, when this is not really a place anyone wants to visit?

The answer is that people don't know any better. They need to be reminded, and sometimes taught, that being a good and kind person is paramount in life, and fighting, hatred and bitterness are to be avoided at all costs. If you have ever experienced the emotional torment of fighting after separation – the pain, the hurt and the sheer cruelty it can bring – I would not believe you if you told me you would prefer that over peace.

So then, why is it that so many couples choose this? I believe it's because they really don't know there is another path, or they don't know how to find it, or they don't know how to stay on it.

The problem we have is that when a couple separates, negative thoughts and actions follow. Your friends, parents or siblings, who always have your back and your best interests in mind, encourage you to 'stand up for yourself' and not to 'roll over' and to 'take them for all you deserve'. So, we instinctively think it's war we need to declare and there is no way to peace.

The flow-on effect from fighting is bad behaviour, arguments, greater feelings of loss and loneliness and – ultimately – a relationship completely destroyed. Kids suffer; they hear and see terrible behaviour between parents who once loved each other and now can't stand the sight of each other. Bank balances suffer as huge amounts of time and money are invested into this fight, and mental health deteriorates. So many parts of people's lives destroyed.

I have seen hundreds of couples in my career wanting to manage their separation in a calm way. But even a mature and carefully-thought-out decision to part after many years of unhappiness can end up with fighting for years in court, resulting in spending thousands, if not hundreds of thousands, of dollars and not being able to look at or even speak to each other by the end of the ordeal.

How did that happen? How can you go from a calm and mutual decision to pure hate and bitterness?

I know this is not what anyone wants. No one wants to go down the hateful path; they really just want to sort things out and move on to a better life. That is usually the very reason that they separated in the first place: they don't want to hate, to fight, and waste all their time, emotion and hard-earned money.

So, what is it that's stopping this from happening? *They are.* Their behaviour. Their decisions. Their actions. Their *choices*.

Their *choice* to fight and not live in peace.

It's time to make a better decision

I assume you are reading this book because you or someone close to you has separated. I further assume that it's your wish to find the most peaceful path possible. It is your time to choose.

Don't behave badly.

Don't be cruel.

Don't argue.

Don't fight.

Stop blaming your ex-spouse or others around you. Stop listening to everyone else. Every action you *choose* to take is yours. No one has the power to make your separation calm and peaceful but you.

Be aware of your actions and your behaviour and the impact this is having every time you make a decision. You need to use your values to guide you, to think deeply about what you really need and what is going to make your life easier.

You also need to be well informed about the options available to you which do not involve a fight. Options that do not include the negativity and hatred surrounding a contested matter.

If you can follow those values, create your own path, be prepared and have all the knowledge and support you need, you will be better placed to make the right decisions to keep you on that peaceful pathway.

The Peaceful Pathway

I know every situation is different – there is different pain and anguish following a separation, different stories, different circumstances. We all feel and think different things, and all go through different stages of this painful phase in our life. It is how we get through it that matters, and who we come out as on the other side.

I get it. I've been there. I was a child of separation, and I myself separated over 10 years ago. It is so very hard. In fact, I would say it is devastating. We all marry thinking that this is *it*. That we love this person so very much and can't imagine ever separating. Sadly, it still happens. It happens to so many people.

My experiences with my own separation and that of my childhood make me who I am today. I am a strong person. I am also a good person. I love to care for people. I believe kindness is the strongest virtue a person can have. I believe my purpose is to look after families and make things easier for them.

That is why I started working in family law. Sadly, after a while I felt I was no longer helping. I was on a legal path that I was trained in and diligently followed, thinking I was doing the right thing. I wrote letters on behalf of clients fighting for their rights, I went to court, trying to make sure that my client received everything they were entitled to. Standing up for them.

About two years ago I realised this was not helping; the problems were getting bigger. In fact, I felt I was *adding* to their problems. I was being criticised for being too kind, when apparently, I should be harsher. That to me was ludicrous. You can never be too kind.

I knew things needed to change for me and the way I worked.

I have absolute respect for the need in some situations for people to pursue their legal rights. I respect the courts and legal professionals that uphold this legislation, but I don't believe it is the only way. It should be a last resort, not a first choice.

The amicable couples work out their own needs, their own issues, and then create a solution that works for their unique family. Why can't other couples?

Well, they can. And it's really not that hard. The hard bit, the part that usually stops them, is bad behaviour and letting emotions take over. Bad choices.

After moving into mediation and collaborative work, I discovered that if clients can behave, can genuinely consider their spouse and stay calm, they can sit down together and talk. When I prepared them for their discussions and made sure they had all the issues set out and the information they needed, they often worked it out themselves.

So, here is where I want to help you. While working with my clients, I have created my own collaborative mediation process. It is a step-by-step process that calms my clients, prepares them, and walks them through a peaceful path towards amicable and peaceful solutions. It utilises the mediation process and the collaborative process all in one. Couples can follow this process too, with or without me.

I have written this book to help couples work through this process on their own. Couples who don't want a fight, who are looking for that peaceful pathway to the end of their separation, but just need a guide, a little help.

By the end of the book not only will you have a solution to your family law problems, you will have a relationship with your ex-spouse that is intact and you will be proud of your actions and behaviour.

This is what I call The Peaceful Pathway.

So, there you go: I can guide you along the way, but it is up to you. You really are the only one who can do this. You choose your path and choose your future. It's never easy, but it can be done.

So why should you listen to me?

I mentioned in the introduction that I too have experienced separation. I have been there; I have lived it. I was 11 years old when my parents separated; at that time peace was the furthest thing from their minds. After the fighting and arguing stopped, my mum left, and my three brothers and I were left with my Dad. I say *left*, as I don't think that anyone really made a choice. My mum just left, and this was the best way she saw to do it. Now this is the view of an 11 year old; now that I am older I realise there was more to it than that, but aren't we wanting to know what our kids are feeling and thinking at these times?

I've been there …

Have you ever had a conversation with someone or overheard someone talking badly about their ex-spouse? In front of the kids? What did you think when you heard it? I know it is something I truly hate. It is a pure example of negative behaviour.

I love my dad dearly; he looked after the four of us children on his own. But he really is an example of what *not* to do and what *not* to say. I think the sadness and the reality of the situation took over his better judgement and he choose negativity, as so many people do.

Dad remarried a few years later, and my brothers and I were introduced to a new family which included my stepmother and her son. Between the two of them, they were my perfect example of 'what not to say in front of children'. I will say, with as much love as possible, that they were my inspiration for not wanting families to suffer like ours did. I am not blaming them – perhaps they didn't know better – but I believe if they had been able to draw upon the assistance and guidance that is available now, things may have been different.

Their behaviour and attitude, despite what they may think, was not helpful. It did not make us better people, it did not make us like them more than her, and yes it made our lives more complicated and traumatic. I honestly think that if they had encouraged our relationship with our mother, even if they didn't like her, our entire world would have been different. There is no blame here, just sadness that their behaviour and their words had such an impact on our lives. I just want others to realise that as a child of separation, the best thing I think my parents could have done for me was be kind to each other, and not fight.

... twice

Now just so you don't think I am still an 11-year-old child not knowing what she is talking about, I can say that not only did I experience separation as a child, but I did so as a 30-year-old woman. This totally devastated me. The sadness and pain I experienced was nothing like I felt as an 11 year old. I now understood. However, my experiences as a child gave me the insight into what was happening and what this would mean for my own children.

I met my husband when I was 16 and he was 19. We were incredibly young. We lived together for some time and married when I was just 23. When we got married, I promised myself that I would never separate. Never. I would not allow my children to feel what I had felt. Life, however, did not agree.

When my babies were just five and three, my husband and I separated after a difficult couple of years. There was so much pain and hurt, so much sadness. So, when I see my clients sitting in front of me crying uncontrollably, crushed, I truly mean it when I say I understand. At the time, I really didn't know how to act, how to respond to situations, what conversations to have. If only I had someone who could have helped me and guided me to do it in the best possible way.

What I did have was common sense and love for my children. Whenever I was faced with a challenge, I would come up with a solution that would create as little impact on my children as possible. I would not say I hid them from the situation, but I would say that

I sheltered them from difficult times and avoided allowing them to see any conflict.

On reflection I think that what I did was choose forgiveness and kindness instead of letting the anger and hurt engulf me. I'm sure you have experienced situations when anger gets the better of you and you choose to yell and scream at the other person, even if it is in front of your kids. Well, somehow I drew on all my strength and I wouldn't do that; I remained silent, I spoke softly and calmly, and if it was really hard to the point where I didn't trust my emotions, I just didn't respond at all. We can all do that; we can choose how we react and respond.

Now please don't get me wrong; nothing is perfect. I know I wasn't. But we need to do our best. There are times when things get hard, but what I remind myself of is that my actions impact on my children, so whatever I say or do must be in their best interests, and I want them to be proud of me one day.

I explain my experience only so that that you know when I say, I understand, I truly do on a personal level.

I have seen it all

In addition to my personal experience I have spent the last 15 years of my professional life dealing with families who are going through exactly the same thing. I am at a stage where I can honestly say *I have seen it all*. The good, the bad and the ugly.

When I was a junior lawyer I was taught to follow a system: we engage the client, obtain numerous and tedious pieces of information, and then we move onto preparing a five- to six-page (sometimes longer) letter that sets out the parties' history, their contributions, and in a neat little table tells them what they now own. Then we negotiate by correspondence; parties get offended, the negotiations fail, and we threaten court.

I think I went on doing this for a good 12 years. I then started to question the effectiveness of this procedure. Why did almost every response I received appear aggressive and negative? No matter how 'nice' I tried to be, there was a sense of aggression and threat in any response. This would upset me as a lawyer and a human; surely it would upset the client so very much more.

In hindsight, I guess I feel a little silly, perhaps naive, that I just accepted that this is the way that family law should be done; who am I to question it? Why change it? Well, over time I gained the confidence to say, *no, this is just not right*. Who wants to be told what they did or did not contribute to the creation of their family's assets? Who wants to be told what their future will and should look like by a stranger? This does not actually help families, it creates more problems, so how can I change this?

What did I do? I left my lovely, safe partnership to venture out on my own and do it my way. I created a fresh start. I created Flourish Family Law. A kind and peaceful way that does not involve courtrooms and nasty letters. I choose to use calm methods such as mediation, collaborative practice, and kinder negotiation techniques. I utilised these practices, and started working on what I call a collaborative mediation process. My own process.

Again, do not be mistaken; I do not believe that this always works for everyone, for every couple. I know that there are so many couples out there that need and benefit from using litigation lawyers and really need the court's assistance and protection, but there are so many more couples who use that pathway as they think it is the only way they have to do it. They are who I am talking to, who I am appealing to; they are my people. They are the ones I am here to help, and educate that there is a kind and calm way to separation.

The journey I believe in follows kind and calm methods, focuses on behaviour, preparation, family and values, and most of all good choices. I am not giving you legal advice, nor am I pushing you to or away from strictly following your legal rights. I am explaining how you can follow a pathway that is linked to the guidelines set out within the legal pathway, but all the while being able to stay calm and creating a solution that will suit you and your family in a positive way, rather than a textbook legal solution.

If this is you, let me take you on that journey.

What is The Peaceful Pathway anyway?

If you are still reading, it means one of two things: you and your partner have separated and you both want to proceed in a kind and calm manner, or you want to learn how to engage your partner and lead them onto a kind and calm path with you and you need help getting them onto that path with you.

Right now, you are probably highly emotional – you have heard a lot of stories, have had lots of opinions offered, and you are totally confused. So, what is the Peaceful Pathway and does it exist in reality? Yes, it does; I have seen it and experienced it. It is not an easy journey but is definitely a rewarding one.

The definition of peaceful is very clear to most. We all know what it is and what it means. Freedom. Tranquillity. Calmness. The list can go on. Now I know, I love and enjoy all of those things, and I am pretty sure most people do. So, how do those things make you feel? Content. Happy. Calm. All great things.

What is the opposite of peace? Conflict and fighting. What do those words mean to you? Distress. Agitation. Hatred. War. I know when I hear those words and think of them invading my life, I am not happy, nor calm.

When we convert those words into a family law setting the effect is similar. If you create a peaceful path then you will feel calm, happy and content. This will not only impact on you and your own health and wellbeing but that of your ex-spouse and your children. Life seems much nicer despite a difficult situation.

If we end up in a family law situation that thrives on the negative aspects, you feel distressed, agitated and upset. These negative thoughts and feelings then have a negative impact on your physical and mental health and also that of your family.

So why would we choose the second option if we can avoid it? The reason this so often happens is because we honestly don't know any better and no one tells us otherwise.

When a relationship ends we are automatically programmed to think negative thoughts; these thoughts then manifest into negative actions and lead to negative outcomes. We almost immediately run to a lawyer, often a lawyer who is only taught to protect your interests at all costs, to run litigation and fight for you. Then you simply get caught up in the whirlwind and don't question your behaviour and why you are writing these litigious letters and threating court action at your ex.

Once you are on that path, feeling there is no other way forward, the entire relationship breaks down from there. You participate in bad behaviour, negativity, even sometimes cruelty and anger. After that, it is very difficult to get back to a peaceful place.

The Peaceful Pathway is quite simple; it is the exact opposite of the situation that I just explained. It involves calm, careful and planned decisions. It utilises positive and effective assistance from others, and it helps you avoid litigation and make good and positive choices following separation.

My experience both personal and professionally has given me the knowledge and experience to be able to see the biggest mistakes that can be made and how to avoid them. Although in my ideal world there is one perfect path, this may not always be the one that couples end up on as a result of other outside mitigating factors; there are many versions of the Peaceful Pathway. My goal is to help you follow the best possible path, using forgiveness, kindness and common sense, to create a future that works best for you.

A peaceful pathway.

Staying on the Peaceful Pathway immediately after separation

What I am about to say is crucial. This is where I want to grab you and sit you down and give you information before you take any drastic action. This is the stage where we all need to stop and think about what we are doing and why. This should happen to all couples immediately after they separate. Stop. Do not make any rash decisions, stay calm, behave and be kind, gather information and plan.

Let's look at it like this: you have just separated and all you know, and all you are told, is that you need to immediately engage a lawyer, the best lawyer, the *toughest* lawyer. You have never had to see a lawyer before, or it has only been to buy a house or make a will; you are fretting because you don't know how to choose one, you don't know what to ask, you feel you will lose everything if you don't go see one right now!

Ask yourself this question. Do you *really* need to get legal advice right now and take action? Is there really something that is immediately pressing? Have you been kicked out of your home, your children taken? If not, perhaps there really isn't an urgent need for legal help right now. Is legal advice really what you need, or is it just information you need? Are there more important things you could be doing first?

I say yes, there are so many more important things. You need to take care of yourself, your kids, and simply stay calm. You need to find out what options you have besides taking legal action. You need a plan, *then* you can see a lawyer if you still feel the need.

Where do you want to go from here? I ask you right now to take a good look at the path ahead:

- **Option one:**

  Involves taking legal action, possible protracted litigation and long legal letters, derogatory and inflammatory statements, spending lots of money on lawyers and time in court – yet that is the path most people follow.

- **Option two:**

  Is calm, takes little time, only uses legal advice where needed, costs less, and is one where you as a couple can create an ideal solution for your family moving forward.

Right now, you can choose.

What if you really do need legal advice?

There are some people who will need to get some legal advice early on. Remember, this can still be peaceful – the key is to choose the right person.

Let's say your partner is threatening to kick you out of the house or take the kids, and you have no idea if they can actually do that. Perhaps they have already taken the kids or stopped paying the mortgage? This is when it is suitable to go get some advice. However, I am again going to give you a choice. Choose the right person to help you. You can choose the right lawyer, a kind and calm lawyer.

Over my years I have met many brilliant colleagues who also love to encourage couples on this kind and calm path. There have been so many advances in out-of-court solutions, online settlements, mediators, and collaborative family law. These too could be a path for you, and yes, they fall into the peaceful category. Later there will be a whole section on how to make the right choice if you *do* need to see a lawyer.

What I am trying to help you do is avoid option one at all steps of this process, unless there is no alternative. You just need to know and understand how to stay on that Peaceful Pathway.

How will this book help me?

It is intended to help couples with or without children. Although some of the stages are relevant to both children and property disputes, I have purposely focused on assisting you with resolving a property dispute.

To do both in the one book was proving to be too much, so perhaps that book may follow.

You will be guided through the various steps to completely prepare yourself, which follows my own standard set of steps used throughout my mediation sessions with clients.

You and your ex-spouse will have a clear idea as to your needs and issues, and will have a set strategy as to what you need in their future. This in itself reduces confusion and conflict. This book will set you up to know and discuss these issues.

You will also be given the knowledge and understanding as to how to prepare your financial records, know what you need and know where to find it. You will be completely ready to discuss these issues, and to move into negotiations whether with your ex-spouse directly or in another peaceful style of negotiation.

If you complete the steps, you will be well prepared, guided in the right direction and shown how to follow a peaceful path. This path will lead you to the creation of your own agreement. Your own solution. One that fulfills all of your issues and needs, and will ultimately allow you to move forward into a calm and peaceful future with your ex-partner. I suggest you read the book from start to finish to begin with, so that you understand the issues and can address anything that needs your immediate attention. I then suggest that you go back to the start and work through the steps and the tasks, only moving on to the next one when you are ready.

Ultimately, when you follow this path you will have a positive and clear relationship moving forward, you will feel pride in your actions and behaviour, and be grateful as to how you have treated each other and very proud of the solution you have reached together. You will save a lot of time and money. Most importantly, your children will benefit from a calm and happy environment and thrive moving forward.

What are the benefits of the Peaceful Pathway?

If you are able to create a calm and peaceful path following your separation then you will see so many benefits, not just for you but for your family and your family's future. These benefits can be short term and long term.

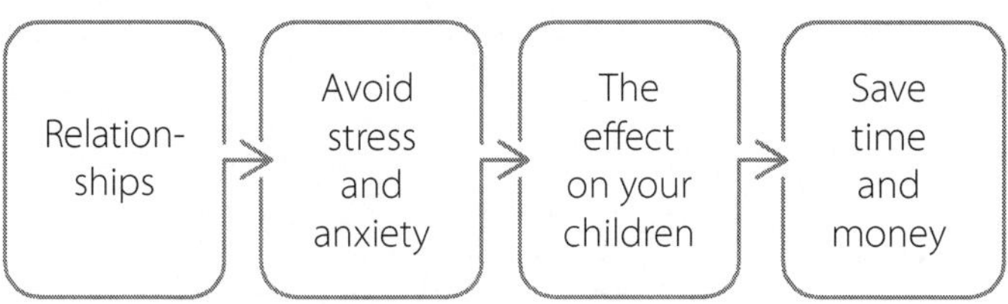

A better relationship with your ex-spouse

This is truly the most important benefit, and can impact every aspect of your new life. If you can have a good relationship with your ex-partner moving forward, almost every aspect of your life will be positively affected. You will be able to have face-to-face, open discussions about your children, and spend time at school or family events without feeling uncomfortable. Even just your day-to-day conversations will benefit.

Imagine your child's first day of school. If you and your ex are in the middle of litigation or have been through litigation, chances are you can't even make eye contact. You are embarrassed by things you have said, so are they. You could still be angry or hurt. There is not a lot of interaction that is going to take place. So, who is going to organise the first day of school? Are you going to go together or separately? Are you going to get joint photos or individual ones?

Look a little further forward; what about graduations or weddings? Do you need to sit separately? My parents can't even sit at the same table together, and in my eyes that is truly sad and difficult for everyone involved. I don't know about you, but I know that it is a horrible feeling.

Let's flip the scenario: what if you had just separated and you were both able to sit down together, talk it out, work together for a solution, be kind and calm with each other? There were no harsh words, no yelling, no derogatory letters, or court, no fighting. These memories and experiences would look completely different for you and for your children.

You may not be best friends, but you can certainly work out who will sit where and who will be in what photo. You and your kids will truly benefit from this. Relationships are everything; it is the way the world works. Without relationships we would have nothing, so why fight and make a relationship that will always be part of your life a difficult one? Fight for a good relationship, not a bad one.

Less stress and anxiety

The clients that I have seen follow a litigious path are often living their day-to-day lives in a state of stress and anxiety. They live in fear of the next argument or even encounter with their ex-spouse. Some people even change their grocery shopping, exercise routine or other daily habits to avoid seeing or running into that person.

The biggest stress I saw in litigation clients was waiting for that dreaded response to a letter that had been sent out. They lived in fear of what was coming next. I have seen clients driven to the point where they had to go on medication just to reduce their levels of anxiety or depression. They needed to seek counselling or use other stress-relief methods.

I once had a client who was required to give evidence in the witness box; she was so upset that the magistrate allowed her to take a break. She went to the bathroom, and after she didn't come out, I went in to look for her. I found her lying on the floor, crying. She was in such a state of distress that we ended up having to call an ambulance and she was taken to hospital. Needless to say, this was one of the most difficult and saddest moments of my career.

Separation itself, even if it is not particularly eventful, is so very stressful and emotional. The fighting and conflict only add to the situation and make everything so very much harder.

To follow a peaceful path after separation, you are taking one massive leap towards avoiding extra stress and extra pain, and taking care of your mental health and wellbeing.

A positive effect on your children

Distressed children is the most common negative effect I see after fighting. However, for those clients of mine led down a peaceful pathway, this has been where we have seen the most positive of effects too.

Just last month I saw a couple who were clearly using their children as a pawn in their arguments. It even got to the point that the dad was arranging to see the child for a special day together, but in response the child was sending terrible text messages to the father telling him he was 'worthless' and a 'cheater' and just a 'scumbag' and that her mother had 'no money to look after them now even though he earns $12,000 a month'. Such adult language.

Now, I know myself that when my children were just 10 years of age these are not words they would have known, let alone voluntarily said to a parent. It may not be that the mother told the child to send such a message, but where did the child hear that language? How would they know how much their father earns a month? The only place that can come from is an adult saying such things in their vicinity.

The result? Severe damage for that family. The father was devastated to the point he was about to give up on seeing his daughter, and I can only imagine how the child will feel looking back on that in a few years. So sad.

My answer? Do *not* do this. Do not talk badly about the other person, no matter how careful you think you are being. Do not discuss your finances in front of the children either. Kids are little sponges; they hear and see everything.

What do you think the outcome would have been for this family had the mother not said those things, or at the very least ensured the child did not hear it? The child certainly would not have repeated these words. Hopefully, what would have happened was the father having a lovely day with his daughter and neither of them having to experience that trauma in their relationship.

Another common example of a child being used as a pawn is the parent who tells the child how lonely they will be when they are with the other parent. How sad and miserable they are when they are alone. For the sake of your child, you need to encourage them to see the other parent; if you are sad, do not tell them that. This can only cause stress and confusion for your children.

It is well known and documented that separation can have a severe long-term effect on children. Your fighting and speaking terribly to each other will only make it worse. Research shows that following a separation, children are twice as likely to have emotional, social and behavioural issues compared to children whose families are still together. If you fight in front of your children, not only will your ongoing relationship with your ex-spouse be affected, so will your children.

Time and money saved

In my experience, two of the most important things to people in life, besides relationships and families, are time and money. We all have precious little time in our busy lives, and we really want to spend our money on things that we enjoy and that make us happy.

This is why I always wonder why so many people very willingly part with these precious things. I have seen so many clients spend thousands of dollars of their hard-earned money on legal fees and spend years of their life in court or in their lawyer's office. It is really simple; if you remain peaceful, stay calm and follow the process, the chances of you wasting large amounts of time and money are significantly reduced.

Each person's or couple's experiences will be different as to the amount of time they spend and the costs they incur. The legal steps can be broken down into a few stages. The cost estimates below are generalised only and are an average amount spent – you will find some lawyers are cheaper and some much more expensive.

Just to give you a guide, the general initial advice and preparation step may cost you $5000. This is just to get some general advice on your rights and responsibilities under the Family Law Act.

You then move into a negotiation phase. If you have a difficult situation, the time your lawyer needs to spend will increase, and so will your fees. If it's smooth, this may cost you anywhere from a further $5000 to $10,000. If not, it will escalate.

If you reach an agreement then you will likely arrange to have your agreement documented, and you will spend a further $2000 to $10,000 to do this depending on complexity.

So, just to get through the basic process, you can be spending anywhere from $7000 to $20,000 and it can take several months, or even over a year.

If you do not reach agreement, here's where the cost can escalate. If you are led through the court system, I have had clients spend anywhere from $10,000 minimum for a very simple case (remembering they have already spent a few thousand on advice and initial negotiations) to $200,000 on their legal fees and expenses. The time it takes to do this can be anywhere from 12 months to five years.

The basic point to make here is that your fees can range anywhere from as little as $5000 to $200,000 depending on what path you take.

If this money were not being spent on legal fees, where would it be spent? It would be in your account, in your investments, or being spent on your children and family. If you can avoid it, why would you choose to spend your money on legal fees if you don't have to? You need to fight to save your time and money.

* * *

After seeing all the benefits, are you wanting to fight to save your relationships, your children's wellbeing, time and money? My process can certainly help you on that path. I have tried and tested this process with my own clients and it really works. This book is written with the aim that you can do most of this yourself, and some things with a little extra assistance.

What are the ingredients to the Peaceful Pathway?

These three ingredients are essential to any peaceful path. It is all up to you. This is a human and personal problem that can be solved in a human and personal way; it is not just a legal problem.

Behaviour + The right team + Preparation = Peaceful Path

Ingredient 1: Behaviour

If you set the stage using kind and calm behaviour, this will create the right environment. From the very minute you separate you need to be very aware of your behaviour and your actions, and question everything you do and why you are doing it. If you can show your ex-partner you can be peaceful no matter the circumstances, they will hopefully follow.

The first thing we need to place our trust in is our own behaviour and our ability to be true to ourselves. You need to reflect on and make clear what your values are, your morals and your interests. What do you need not just to survive, but to thrive also?

Kindness, in my book, is the strongest value that will take you a long way in any separation. Calmness is the next best attribute. If you can stay calm, collect your thoughts, consider your behaviour and not be reactive, you are way ahead.

Ingredient 2: The right team

You need to choose the right people to be part of your team. Learn how to choose people who understand you, who want to help you reach a resolution and guide you in a positive and peaceful way. I cannot express this strongly enough, and will continue to say this again and again, but the people you choose to walk this path with, to get advice from along the way, are so important – a key ingredient.

You need to follow your values and morals, and select the right person whom you trust and feel comfortable with to give you advice. A person who is in line with your values, someone who has your best interests at heart and who will understand you as a person, not just as a legal problem.

Ingredient 3: Preparation

Preparation helps you avoid confusion, mistakes and uncertainly. Being fully knowledgeable and prepared is your final key. If you have everything you need to be informed, and have the necessary knowledge and understanding, you will reduce confusion, misunderstandings and of course arguments.

* * *

If you can use these three traits and follow my steps, you will find the peaceful path.

The Peaceful Pathway process

I am sure by now you are wondering how this actually works. How does the Peaceful Pathway work? What is the most peaceful way forward?

Well, it is up to you. You get to choose. Every couple will be different, and the most peaceful pathway for them will also be different.

My passion and my job is to educate and guide couples on the best possible path, the most peaceful path. So, with my help, you can work out the best pathway for you and your family.

As with any theory, although there are some simple ingredients, there also needs to be a process. I have used my process with many mediation couples and it truly works. I have separated the steps of separation into thoughtful stages to make it easy and calm for my clients to follow. If you can fight hard to stay on my path, even on your own, I believe you will have the same outcome: peace.

This is the Peaceful Pathway, which we will be exploring throughout the book:

1. **Stay calm:**

   Realign yourself and your values. Map your new pathway.
2. **Prepare:**

   Do your research. Form your team. Create action lists and consider your needs and interests.
3. **Gather:**

   Collect all the information, documents and advice you need.
4. **Explore:**

   Investigate, fully understand and review your needs. Do a regular reality test to make sure you are still on the pathway.
5. **Negotiate:**

   Create the right atmosphere. Know what you need to discuss. Negotiate. Find ways through your obstacles.
6. **Resolve:**

   Finalise your agreement. Test your solution. Write it up.

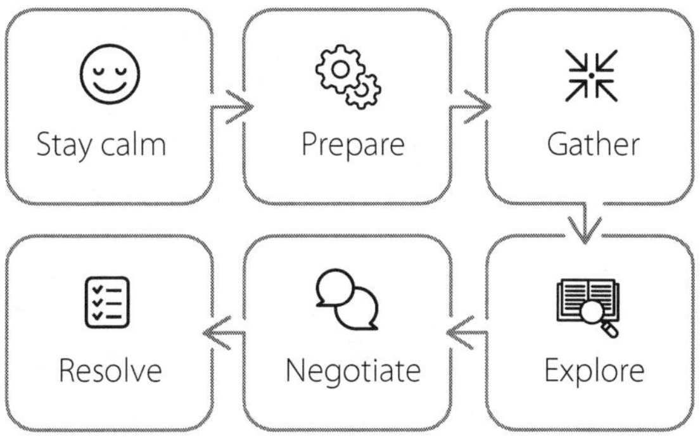

What is an amicable separation?

In my experience, amicable separations occur when the two parties are able to put aside their differences, their emotions even, and work through their issues without fighting. It's about being able to face each other and talk openly without being accusatory or derogatory. It is a choice. We choose our actions, and you can choose to do the things in this book.

Choosing to be amicable

You can choose to be amicable and you can also choose a team that helps and teaches you how to be amicable.

I know there are so many couples out there who could be on the amicable, kind and calm path, but are not. Why? They are often unaware or are led down the incorrect path by those who advise them.

Last year I took on a client who said she wanted to be amicable, but then she would often allow her emotions to take over and would become downright nasty. It took all my patience and experience to keep her on the right pathway. I knew she was not thinking clearly, and I would often wait to allow her to calm down and get control of her emotions before we would move forward.

Often, I would find she would calm down the next day and change her instructions. She was a kind and sweet lady, but she was highly distressed and angry and it affected her behaviour.

Now, rather than joining in on her destructive path and sending letters and offers that were highly inflammatory (which is what she thought we needed to do), I was able to calm her down, and we took the time to let her review and think about her actions before doing anything.

By following my own values, keeping her calm, and giving her good advice, in the end we were able to reach a good settlement for her. All she really wanted was to make sure she kept her house. She had put so much hard work into it and felt so emotional about it that she often couldn't think straight. We finally reached an agreement, wrote up the documents, and she now has her house.

The reason I remember this matter so clearly is not just because of her difficult behaviour but because I received an email from her husband not long after settlement. He wrote: 'If it wasn't for your kind and calm nature and the way you assisted my wife, we would never have settled this.' He also said, 'for the sake of humanity please keep doing this and don't stop'.

These very words were my inspiration to start writing this book.

If you had asked me a few years ago the ratio of amicable versus disputing couples I had, I would say that it was about 70/30, sadly not in favour of the amicable side. However, once I changed my own mindset and started to follow my own rules and my values and show clients that there can really be an amicable path, my clients became 80% amicable to 20% not so.

How do you convince your former partner to join you?

It is your choice to be amicable; no one can make you do it. If you have made that choice, good on you – you have started down the Peaceful Pathway.

The difficulty is often finding both people in a couple that are choosing to be amicable. I have had hundreds of clients come to me and tell me all they want is a quick and cordial settlement, only to be bitterly disappointed that no matter what we try, their former partner is just not interested in playing along.

If you are wanting to be amicable but you don't think your partner will, don't lose hope. Really think about ways you believe this unique individual, whom you know very well, would be convinced that an amicable pathway is better. If you have all the right information you can share it with them. You can make positive choices and set an example for good behaviour.

What happens if you are ready to move forward in a calm and amicable way, yet your ex-partner is still not interested? Obviously, the answer will be totally different in each situation. I have honestly had thousands of clients over my career and no two couples are the same.

Don't think that you have to behave like someone else, or that your spouse should act like someone you know or have heard of; this is all about you and your ex-spouse and how you both will best individually deal with this process. We cannot force someone to act in a way that we want them to, but we can set a scene, lead by example and respect their individuality to follow the right path.

I will never say that working amicably is for all couples; it is not. There are many situations where domestic violence, mental health issues and family circumstances may not allow for it or it is simply not suitable. In those circumstances, you can still follow a calm path for yourself, which should involve choosing the right lawyer for you (take a look at my section on choosing the right advice).

The first tip in my experience is to watch your own behaviour; if you can set the scene and the best example then you will go a long way. I have a whole section dedicated to how to do this best. In short, in my experience it is very hard for someone to continue to be nasty, derogatory or negative if you aren't.

I have even tested this theory in everyday life. When a family member, friend or colleague is getting upset or angry, rather than letting their arguments or negativity get to me or joining in, I choose to stay calm. Instead of just saying 'no' or arguing just to have my say, I stay calm and ask more questions. Always more questions; information is gold.

Once they have felt heard, the discussion is so much easier.

If you can set the standard of behaviour and be a good listener, letting the other person feel heard, it is more than likely they will do that too.

If you are trying to steer your separation along the amicable path, rather than demanding a certain approach, take your time, talk about it, give your partner the information and the benefits, and set the standard of behaviour. Nine times out of ten they – eventually – follow.

Finally, please remember, amicable doesn't have to be the two of you doing it alone. It can be done in other ways; look at all your other options. Just knowing them and choosing the best one for you and your ex-spouse can still be more peaceful than the fighting.

Characters

To show you the various ways we can be calm and peaceful, throughout my book I am going to introduce you to five couples. They are made-up names and characters but realistic stories; they are certainly not the exact stories from couples, but have aspects that I have worked with over my years as a lawyer. In each case I have changed the stories and circumstances slightly, but I wanted to introduce you to them so you can see how very different each pathway can be.

You will find their respective stories woven throughout the book as you take the journey yourself through the steps of the Peaceful Pathway.

Step 1
Stay calm

'Panic causes tunnel vision.
Calm acceptance of danger allows us to more easily
assess the situation and see the options.'

Bestselling author Simon Sinek

How to start creating your very own pathway

If you have just separated and you are reading my book, I will assume you are searching for a calm and peaceful way forward.

Step 1 is all about staying calm – realign yourself with your values, your moral compass, learning not take any drastic action when it is not necessary, and allowing time to map out your own pathway. Your fight here is to keep calm.

The key to staying calm and aligning yourself is following a few simple steps.

The first thing most clients say to me when they separate is that they have no idea where to start – they are stressed, anxious and lost. That is perfectly okay. No one really knows where to start. You are not expected to be an expert on the process of separation, or have all the answers.

Just by reading this book you are taking your first step on the Peaceful Pathway. Here are the stages to help you stay on track.

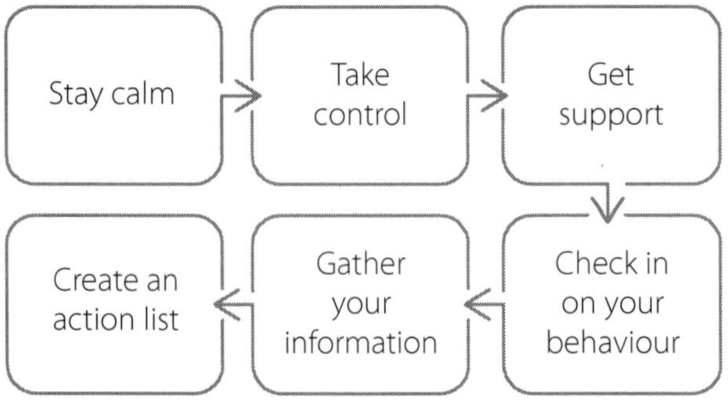

Step 1 of my process is not about getting legal advice (which is what everyone always assumes comes first), it is about knowing what advice you really do need, when you need it, and where to find it. It is also about making sure you are in the right frame of mind to start the process.

So, before you make an appointment to get advice, you need to calm yourself, and make no major moves or decisions – find all of the information and support you need first. If you do, *you* can set your path and decide what advice *you* do need, not anyone else.

The importance of staying calm

The reason I use the word 'calm' is for me that is the best way to describe how you should act. Do not be reactive, do not be aggressive, do not use your emotions to make your decisions.

If you can stay calm you will be able to carefully and thoughtfully place yourself, and your family, in the best possible position to move forward positively. You will be able to carefully and clearly review all of your options before taking action.

I recently had a couple who came to me a few days after they had separated. The wife, in a very reactive manner, had the very next day after separation phoned a lawyer she looked up online, made an appointment and sought some advice. Within 24 hours of seeking this advice, the lawyer (without the wife approving this, mind you) sent the husband a demanding letter setting out the history of their relationship, included all of his mistakes, and telling him that if he didn't disclose his financial position within 14 days then legal action would be taken. As you could expect, this letter completely threw him into a fit of rage; he was upset, angry and hurt. Well, if I had received this letter, I would freak out too. What he did do right was he called me to ask for help. He didn't simply fight back.

He said to me that he really didn't understand why he had received this letter; he said he had no idea what financial disclosure was, why he had to do it, and what he even needed to supply. He really did not want to go to court, and had no idea how this horrible demand had come about. He thought he and his wife had separated on the best possible terms, and it had only been a few days before.

So, I told him to stay calm. I then gave him my usual advice about his options and responsibilities moving forward, without giving legal advice at this point, and I suggested that perhaps he have a talk with his wife about whether this was the path that she wanted to go down. I gave him a little more information about the options so that he could have a chat to her and see what she thought.

Within an hour he had phoned me to say that his wife was totally horrified. She had gone to seek some advice but had no idea as to the contents of that letter, and very clearly said this was *not* the path she wanted to go down. Needless to say, she phoned the lawyer immediately and advised that she no longer required her services.

Within two weeks they were booked in for mediation, and have very calmly started the process. In the very first meeting they worked out what they wanted to do with their interim finances, were explained the process calmly and clearly, and also agreed what they would do with the care of the children.

The key here is that perhaps if she had kept calm, not freaked out immediately after separation and sought immediate legal advice (or had instead sought the *right* advice), she may have taken a very different path.

Communication and information are the key. It is essential to stay calm and plan. Think about it; if the husband had simply responded to this inflammatory letter, like I have seen many do, by engaging his own lawyer to respond immediately, this couple would most likely have been very soon fighting in the court system. Such a totally different outcome.

Your immediate response as to how to deal with the separation – and the choices as to how you behave, and who you choose to help you – is so important. It will set your pathway. Carefully thought out and researched choices will set you on a positive path. Rash and urgent actions often lead to destruction.

I would now like to introduce my first couple to you.

Couple 1: Trish and Marcus (litigation)

Trish and Marcus have been married for 10 years; they have a boy and a girl, aged 8 and 10. They own a local sheep farm and Marcus manages the farm. Trish also works on the farm to help Marcus when he needs it, to help feed shearers, assist with stock, and she also kept the farming books. Trish was an accountant but was only working casually. She preferred to be able to be home for the kids during the week and spent a lot of time on the farm – they found it too hard if she worked full time.

Trish and Marcus had always had a troubled relationship; they had broken up a couple of times before they got married, but ultimately got back together and then had the kids. But things just got worse as the kids got older, and Trish decided she could not cope any longer and told Marcus that she had to leave. She told him late one night, and Marcus agreed but said that he was not leaving – she would need to.

The day after she told him it was over she arranged a moving van, and when Marcus was not at the house, she took a large majority of the furniture. She had arranged a rental property and set herself up there.

Upon returning, Marcus was livid to find the house almost bare; she had left one bed, the kitchen table, and the fridge. Most of the furniture was gone. So, Marcus, without thinking, called her and left an abusive message. Trish did not answer, knowing what it would be about, so Marcus then sent a text telling her what he thought of her. Trish, again without thinking about the consequences, sent one just as horrible back. And so, the negative cycle began.

While all of this was going on, Trish also transferred $50,000 from their farming account into her own personal account.

What happened here was that neither party was able to keep themselves calm. Their emotions and the stress took over and they ended up taking drastic actions that significantly hurt and impacted the other. Neither of them stopped to think about the long-term effects of their actions and did not get any assistance, information or guidance before they acted.

Taking control

After being able to calm yourself, you will need to take control of the situation. Take time to look at what information you need and figure out where you will find it.

Before you start taking furniture, transferring money, calling lawyers and writing letters of demand, make sure you really know what it is you are after. Learn and research what all your options are. What are you wanting a lawyer to do? Are you fully prepared and ready to start this process? Do you even need a lawyer yet?

No one really knows the answers to these questions immediately after they separate. To help guide my clients, I have created the Peaceful Pathway so that they can calmly and carefully move through a process.

You can very easily follow this process, and if you do, you will not only have a clear picture about what you need to do, but you will not go down that negative pathway where you spend thousands of dollars on litigation and years in court and forever destroy your relationship through bad and embarrassing behaviour.

Sound good? Okay, let's get you started.

Time to align and prepare yourself

Get support

The first thing you must do is take care of yourself. If you are not well or healthy, mentally and physically, you will struggle to achieve anything and your ability to make good decisions will be highly impaired.

Some people following separation are a mess. I had a recent client who told me she cried for seven days straight, had sleepless nights, and had no motivation or will to even live. She just could not function and could not continue like this. So, we arranged support for her. There is no way she could make good decisions about what action to take. She needed to get herself right first.

Others are affected less and can cope, some only to fall over a few months later. We are all different. We all go through the stages of grief at different times following separation and often at different times to our ex-partner. No matter what stage you are at, you will always benefit from having support, love and care around you. So why not set up those networks now?

Choose the right people

Be honest with your family and friends, tell them what you need from them, how they can or cannot help and have them in place, just in case you need them. Have a really good think about who your 'go-to person' is who can calmly and rationally best assist you at this time. Choose wisely.

I am not saying you can't talk to more than one friend or family member, but it truly helps to have that one person who you can ask to help keep you on track. You really don't need that beautiful but aggressive friend right now who wants to tear your ex-spouse apart. Look for the level-headed, practical person who knows you very well. We need the calm and rational person, not the fighter.

If you are not feeling yourself or are struggling to cope with a recent separation, make an appointment as soon as possible to see your GP. Your GP can even refer you to a counsellor or psychologist for support to help you get some assistance if needed. Do not think that this means you are a failure and cannot cope; this is putting in place your support networks.

Take care of yourself

What things make you feel good or help clear your mind? Meditation, walking, yoga, running, massage. Whatever they are, now is the time to draw on these things. You need to make sure that you are taking care of yourself and caring for yourself. If you are not healthy, you cannot make life-impacting decisions, or if you do, I'm sure they won't be good ones.

Eat and sleep well

Rest and food are essential. It is amazing how many people forget that they need to do these basic things after they separate. Again, if you are struggling with this and need advice, go to your GP, get support, and get your body right before you move forward.

What resources are available?

Family counselling

I encourage many families to engage in family counselling. There are a range of options to assist individuals, couples and families during marriage, separation and divorce.

They will assist you with many things. The aim is not necessarily to get you back together (unless that is what you are wanting); it is to help you cope with the separation, assist you to develop positive ways to move forward, to help you come up with parenting solutions or talk about parenting issues.

Try these two low-cost organisations to get started:

- www.familyrelationships.gov.au
- www.relationships.org.au

I commonly send clients to counselling before we start the process. To access private family counsellors, you can find one yourself online or through recommendations. You can also try www.healthdirect.gov.au or talk to your doctor and seek a referral.

Courses

There are a lot of great programs that have been developed to assist you after separation. Some people choose to use both a counsellor and enrol in such courses. I have seen great benefits come from this.

The courses are designed to improve communication and personal resilience regardless of who is causing conflict in the relationship.

You can research some courses at:

- www.betterrelationships.org.au
- www.relationshipsnsw.org.au/support-services/parenting-after-separation-focus-on-kids
- www.relationshipsnsw.org.au/support-services/flying-solo
- www.parentingafterseparation.com.au

Support services

Another great resource is your local Family Support Service. Not all areas have one, but through these you can access counselling, courses and other resources such as parenting groups to help you.

The government site Family Relationships Online – Helping Build Better Relationships at www.familyrelationships.gov.au also has a lot of great information and publications to send you in the right direction.

Let's take at look at our second couple we will follow, Jennifer and William.

Couple 2: Jennifer and William (one with a good lawyer, one without representation)

Jennifer is 30 and William is 32. They have two very young girls, aged 3 months and 18 months. William is a stay-at-home dad, previously having worked in sales, but is on Workers' Compensation for a back injury, and Jennifer is a beautician. Jennifer works five days a week from 8am until 4pm. Jennifer and William met when they were young but were just friends at first. After about seven years however, things changed, and they moved in together. Not long after that they had their first daughter. They never married as neither was very interested in doing so.

Jennifer has been unhappy for some time, and she has recently realised that she just cannot continue to be in this relationship. She and William fight constantly about the house; she doesn't think that he does enough around the house and is constantly unhappy with the diet he gives the girls while she is at work. They just argue constantly, and it's getting worse and Jennifer just wants out. She tells William this and explains that she is going to move out. She has said she would like to look at sharing the care of the girls on a week on–week off arrangement.

William is very unsure about what to do from here. He thinks that a week on–week off arrangement might work, but in all honestly, he is so distressed that Jennifer wants to leave him. He just wants her to stay. He hadn't realised that things were that bad and had no idea she was so unhappy. William seeks some help from his local Family Support Service, and they refer him to a counsellor who can talk with them both. He feels this is the best way to make sure that this is really what Jennifer wants, as he really wants them to just repair things.

Jennifer and William do attend the joint counselling session and try the methods that are given to them by the counsellor. She agrees that they will work at things for another four weeks and she will see how she feels.

After the four weeks, she is still feeling no different, and when they return to counselling she makes it very clear that it is over. She really wants out of the relationship. William is devastated. They agree to go to a few more sessions, but more so to continue with assistance with their co-parenting and how to move forward.

Jennifer is keen to make sure that they maintain a good relationship for the sake of the girls and wants to remain friends if possible.

This couple really utilised good services to help them on their way. They sought clarity and assistance as to how to move forward amicably. This will really set them up for a positive pathway ahead, despite the difficult situation.

I am not sure if I need legal advice right now

Although legal advice may be necessary for you at some point, the question is, at what stage do you need it? This choice can be critical.

If your circumstances do not require any immediate and urgent legal advice, be comfortable knowing that it is okay to remain calm, prepare yourself and gather your information before you do get advice. Wait until later in the process so you can see if it is really needed. Some people find that they do not need any advice until the very end of this process; there is so much of it that they can do alone.

If you do choose to seek legal advice right now, that is still okay. The key here is to choose that person wisely and ensure you ask them to advise you on all the options that are available to you. (Refer to *Step 2: Getting legal advice*, which gives you a clear guide on how best to choose the right person for you.)

Checking in on your behaviour

I have seen it time and time again, and I'm sure I too have participated in bad behaviour; we all do it. If you can, throughout this entire process, check in on yourself and your behaviour; you will be well placed to stay on a peaceful path.

We all know what bad behaviour is and have probably felt the consequences of it in the past. It can show up in many shapes and sizes.

I have had couples come to me saying that they want to sort things out amicably, that they still get along well enough to talk and be in the same room, but then the whole relationship goes downhill. Nine times out of ten this is due to poor behaviour.

Before I work through this with you, I need to explain why this is so very important. Our response and our attitude to all things that arise after a separation are what matters. We need to be aware of what is important. The only way to make change is to take personal responsibility and make things happen. We need to take the initiative to change our behaviour, and be responsible for it, rather than playing the blame game.

The language we use and our mode of communication are so important.

If we sit in a corner and say that 'nothing I do matters' and blame everyone and everything else for the bad things that happen, we will not be able to move forward.

Yes, it may be that someone else's behaviour is bad or has caused your heartache, but what is important here is how you choose to react. This is where you have the power, the power to choose how you respond. Put simply, if you respond to negative behaviour in a negative way, you will get more negative results.

However, if you take control and choose not to be the victim, use proactive language, and take proactive actions by looking for alternative and better ways, you can be in control of the outcomes. You control your feelings, no one else. They may cause you to have feelings, but it is you who chooses the response, so do it your way.

To do this you need to follow your morals and values; don't compromise on your own integrity.

Task 1

Time to start working. I want you to think about and write down what you believe your values to be. What is the moral compass you follow?

Use my examples below, or feel free to add your own.

Accountability. Achievement. Adventure.
Balance. Being the best. Belonging.
Caring. Commitment. Compassion.
Dignity. Diversity.
Efficiency. Equality. Ethics. Excellence.
Fairness. Faith. Family. Forgiveness. Freedom. Friendship.
Generosity. Gratitude. Growth.
Harmony. Honesty. Humour.
Inclusion. Independence. Integrity.
Job security. Joy. Justice.
Kindness. Knowledge.
Leadership. Learning. Love. Loyalty.
Making a difference.
Nurture.
Openness. Optimism. Order.
Parenting. Patience. Peace. Power. Pride.
Recognition. Reliability. Risk taking.
Safety. Security. Self-discipline. Self-respect. Success.
Teamwork. Time. Tradition. Trust.
Understanding. Uniqueness.
Vision. Vulnerability.
Wealth. Wellbeing. Wisdom.

Once you have completed this list, I ask you to circle the three most important values that you have written down.

Mine are: *Kindness. Forgiveness. Honesty.*

Now you have your top three values, I ask that you consider that when checking in on your behaviour, you consider these the utmost values to follow. Consider the best way to respond in accordance with your values. These should be the things that are most important to you, that give you purpose and make you feel good about yourself and others when followed.

These values should best describe or define you. They will be when you feel at your best and are the guide to help you make those hard decisions. Your compass.

After considering and making clear what values define you, let me help show you how following those values can best serve you and how the failure to follow values has not served others.

Jane and Peter are my third couple. Jane has always had a clear sense of her values and this truly assisted her and Peter during their separation.

Couple 3: Jane and Peter (collaborative practice)

Jane and Peter met when they were at high school. They lived in a quiet, small town. Jane was from a wealthy family and Peter lived with his dad; his mother passed away when he was only five years old.

Peter was actually two years above her at school, but when Jane was in year 10, they started dating. Peter finished year 12 but then got an apprenticeship as a mechanic so stayed in town and lived with his dad.

Sadly, Jane's parents did not agree with their relationship, so she ultimately left her parents' home, and while she was studying year 12 she stayed with Peter and his dad. They had a wonderful relationship and were almost inseparable. When Jane finished school, they moved to Melbourne so that she could go to university to study business and Peter was able to transfer with his job.

Peter was their main income earner and worked full time, while Jane worked hard at studying. They eventually married and had two children, a boy named Justin and a girl named Tabitha. Jane finished her business management degree and found a great job.

Their relationship was steady for some time, but the stress of having two small children did take a toll. Peter continued to work, and Jane took maternity leave to look after the children.

When Justin was 3 and Tabitha 18 months, Jane discovered that Peter was having an affair. She was utterly devastated – although she knew their relationship was not perfect, she never expected something like this would happen. They did try to patch things up again, but after 12 months of giving it a try Jane realised that Peter was still seeing the woman he'd had an affair with, and she ended the relationship.

Now here is where Jane differs from so many other clients I have seen. Our natural response is to cry and scream and abuse the other person. It is a natural reaction of our brain to fight to protect ourselves, but not Jane.

When she discovered what was happening, she calmly called her husband. He did not answer. So, she left a message. She explained to him that she was aware of where he was and what he was doing, and just asked him not to come home. She said she would take the kids out for the day and asked him to come home during the day to collect the things he needed for the next few weeks, and she would talk to him again in a few days so that he can arrange to see the kids. She kindly and respectfully asked him not to call her or try to change her mind as there was just no use.

Well, he didn't call back and he didn't argue. Jane had set the standard of behaviour, and this is where they carried on from. Now their story is not perfect, no one's ever is, but they really are the best example I can give you to show you how this can work for you too.

Jane and Peter really had to think about what they were doing at all times, and sometimes they didn't always choose the best path. Peter was really struggling with the situation and very quickly came to feel guilt for what he had done to Jane. He was struggling emotionally. A friend recommended he go and see a counsellor to help him through his difficult time.

Jane was thinking along a similar path and she also reached out to her local Family Support Service and planned for them both to participate in a parenting program. She felt it would help them both move past this very difficult time and put the kids first.

Jane also used the 'values' method and clearly set out what values she felt were her strongest, as she wanted to make sure she stuck to them throughout this difficult time. Her strongest values were honestly, respect and kindness.

Jane knew she wanted to set a path forward that would follow these values. She had heard that there were alternative methods to negotiations outside of court. She really wanted to avoid court first and foremost. Her good friend had gone through the court system and it was one of the most distressing situations she had witnessed. Her friend was constantly stressed and upset, and her relationship with her ex-husband was totally destroyed. They can't even speak to each other now. It took her friend three years to get it sorted, and although Jane doesn't know how much it cost her, she knows it was a huge financial burden. So, she really didn't want to go down that path.

Jane went ahead and did more research into her options. She didn't think, given the situation, that she and Peter would easily be able to sit down and work things out on their own. She also felt she needed some support during the process. So, she contacted a lawyer who advised that they conduct a collaborative practice. Jane loved the idea of this. She knew that it meant she had legal support, they could contact their accountant where necessary, and that they would still have the opportunity to try to sort this out on their own.

To make this decision and start the calm path, Jane was able to follow her values, which in this case allowed these parties to move forward in a very positive and calm way. I remember seeing the huge impact that this behaviour had on the outcome. Such positive behaviour and a positive path.

Examples of bad behaviour

Text messages

It is most common for separated parties to shoot off a quick text message to communicate. Now this may seem simple and normal, but honestly some of the text messages I have seen, you would never want to read back to yourself a few years later. You would be horrified.

I think the ease of a text message is what causes people to lose the ability to stop and think about what they are writing and how it would be received, or alternatively they are in a state of anger or frustration and their emotions take over and they just type and send. After reading some of these messages I am sure that they have not even read over them. The spelling and grammar are all over the place and they often don't even make sense. Sadly, what then happens is that the receiver has the immediate urge to respond, and then it just keeps going.

What I ask you to do here is that every single time you send a message, take a look at those three values you listed above. Then ask yourself, does this message I am about to send align with those values?

I am not just talking about the creation of a chain of messages; I am talking about the response. No matter how horrible the message – rude, hurtful and upsetting – why respond in the same way if that is not in line with your own values? If you do, you are choosing to act in a way that is different to what you normally would want. Why? Because you were sent a horrible message? If you do not want to fall into that trap, then choose another response. Choose to respond in a way that is appropriate; don't be reactive. If you need to wait before you respond, then do that. Give yourself the time to pull it together and make the right choice.

Clients often say to me, 'well, he sent this message, so I had to respond'. No. No you did not. You *chose* to respond like that. He or she didn't *make* you. He or she did choose to send you that horrible text. Your reaction and response are within *your* control.

It is also important to note that, in my experience, when clients choose to use the positive and calm response, the other party often eventually follows. This may not always happen, and it can at times take longer for some to get the picture, but it usually does happen. The result is a more positive and effective mode of communication to move forward.

At the very least, you will be able to hold your head high and feel pride in the way that you have chosen to respond, even if they didn't always follow your lead.

Emails

Emails are remarkably similar to texts. Anger or resentment sets in, and a nasty or rude email is shot off to the other person without even thinking about it. The problem I see with emails is that they are longer. You can attach things and forward them to other people. I have witnessed some terrible emails in my time. More often than not, texts and emails are also misinterpreted due to tone or words that are used.

What I say to you here is very simar to what I said about texts. In fact, I will repeat this for all forms of communication. Do not respond in a manner that is contrary to your own values. Why? Because you can choose not to and it will calm the situation.

My tip here, which I follow myself, is the 24-hour response rule. If you receive an email that is antagonistic or upsetting, write out your response, put it all in there if it makes you feel better. Then save. Do not send that. Give yourself 24 hours and re-read it. If there is anything in there that is purely reactive and not appropriate, then change it.

Finally, the biggest question to ask yourself is, do I really need to respond to this at all? If the answer is *no, I can call or discuss next time I see them*, then that is often the better way to handle an email.

General conversations

We all have feelings, feelings that can get hurt. We all have reactions. Reactions that are all different. If, however, you can learn how to converse with your ex in a positive and kind manner, your communication and conversations will be so much better.

One-on-one conversations are the best. Text messages and emails can be misinterpreted or taken the wrong way and are often the riskiest. So why not go back to the use of basic face-to-face conversations. You can explain yourself and tell your version correctly. Body language is important here; you can read the other person's reaction and they can read yours.

You need to learn and remember not to react when something upsets you. Carefully consider what is said and respond in the kindest and calmest way possible. Keep your values in mind. Is the response you are about to make in line with those values. Or are you simply being reactive?

The biggest mistake is being reactive in a conversation. If it is getting too much, leave. Don't stand there and yell back at the other person. You can choose to leave the conversation and come back to it. If they are being rude, you can choose to ignore the rudeness, follow your values and be kind and calm back. Not many people will continue to be horrible or rude in the face of kindness. This is hard I know, but you can at least give it a try.

Also look at the use of kindness. You know your ex-partner well; what are the things they will appreciate and will make their life easier? Offer them information that will be of assistance to them. Do they know what time the next soccer games is on or when the school assembly is? Why not tell them if you think they are likely to not know or may forget? These little things will make a big difference.

Social media

I have left this one for last because, in my opinion, it is the worst. In fact, it can be so bad that I have seen social media posts annexed to affidavits to show the court the types of behaviour parties are participating in. Abusive and aggressive photos, words, images – none of them are a good look.

If you are a parent, what do you teach your children about social media usage? I am certain that you would not approve of derogatory remarks or pictures being posted for all the world to see – forever. That is why I am so astonished when I do see what some adults are posting.

This is where you need to go back again to your values. Think about what you are posting. Are you being responsive or antagonistic? Consider whether this is something that could cause the other person pain or start an argument. If the answer is *yes*, then why post it? How does this post advance your life and your wellbeing? Now is the time to be very thoughtful and considerate and smart.

It is not always the nasty posts that cause the problems. I have seen innocent posts cause trouble too. The new girlfriend or boyfriend. A fancy holiday, or even something new with your kids. Does the other person have access to see these posts? Just be considerate.

When it comes to the kids, you should both try to discuss and agree what is appropriate and what is not about your kids. I have some clients who agree to not post any pictures of their kids at all. That solves a lot of problems. Others who love their social media will agree that pictures of kids can be posted but with nothing showing their name, school or other items that could identify them. It is really up to you. You just need to talk about it before you do and make sure that you are both on the same page. If not, wait until you are.

Don't just go ahead and post things that could inflame the situation.

How do you want to behave?

It's time for you to think about *your* best behaviour. I call this creating your own 'behaviour guide'. The reason I get clients to do this is so that they can reflect on the things that make them feel good and also the things that make them feel bad and possibly then behave badly.

I started doing this with clients as they would often say to me that they were struggling to keep their behaviour in check. Think about those strongest values and morals you hold highly; how is it that you expect others to act and behave? How would you like to look back and see yourself behaving?

It is hard; remember what I said before about the stages of separation and grief? When you get to the anger stage it is really hard to stay calm. When you are in sadness, you just want to cry. If you need to create some space and relax before a discussion or making a decision, or go for a walk to unwind after a confrontation, your 'behaviour guide' will help you.

When I am feeling my emotions take over, I use my own best behaviour guide:

> *Always listen and not interrupt. Allow the other to speak. Being a good listener is key. I hold truthfulness first and foremost. So always tell the truth. Don't listen to gossip. Never write, text or say anything that I wouldn't want others to see.*

I actually use this guide in my day-to-day discussions with friends and family. It helps keep me in check when I am having a difficult discussion or am not sure how to deal with something. If I follow this guide, I may not resolve an issue, but I will be happy with the way that I have acted and responded. And if I act in the opposite manner to my guide, I am usually very upset with myself and often feel negative or unhappy thoughts.

Task 2

Create your own behaviour guide. Have a go at writing down your own personal rules. Try to incorporate your morals and values and what behaviour you yourself value the most.

You don't have to have as much or as little as me. Use this list as a best practice guideline as much as possible. You can even create a list on your phone if that makes it more assessable for you; that way you can refer to it or add to it whenever you need to. Start writing down the things that will make your path calmer and those that will make it harder.

The aim of this list is to keep you moving towards using positive behaviours and avoiding the negative ones. If you can see and experience how the use of the positive behaviours and responses works then you will eventually default to them as a first response.

Time to plan

Create an action checklist

So now that you have looked at what support you need and how you can best behave, we can move onto some action and start some planning.

I haven't yet introduced this part of myself, but you may have already started sensing it, and will find it comes out throughout this book: I am a planner. You will find that I will ask you to make plans and lists on a regular basis. Why? Well, who doesn't like a plan? Yeah … okay, not everyone. But plans *are* helpful and will keep you on track. I also believe that if you can write something down and see it, it will make more room in your head for harder things to think about and will make the pathway much clearer for you, so let's get it out of your head. Time to plan together!

What do you need *right now*?

Take some time to sit down and really think about what you need to keep going over the next few weeks. At this point, let's not get too far ahead of ourselves – don't worry about the long-term issues for now. Let's focus on the simple things like arranging some time off or some extra childcare to allow you time to think, relax or run errands.

Also look at your financial needs:

- Do you have any large bills that are coming up and you need extra funds?
- Do you have access to enough savings or income to cover your immediate needs?

- Do you need to make alternative arrangements for work or the kids, or to talk to someone at Centrelink about benefits?
- Perhaps you need to take some time off work or contact your bank?
- Do you need to open a separate account so that your income goes into there now?
- What else do you need to do?

Task 3

Write a list of all the things that you need to do *right now*. I want you to think carefully, and use the following guide to help you along.

Once you have the list created, place the items in order of priority and set yourself a goal to get through them.

Example action list

Priority	Item	Completed
	Apply for leave at work	
	Do you need to open an individual bank account?	
	Do you need to change where your pay or benefits are deposited?	
	Talk to support services and seek financial support with Centrelink	
	Review what bills need to be paid	
	Do names on utility bills need to be updated?	
	If you moved out – mail redirection	
	If you have permanently relocated, you might need to consider updating your driver's licence address	

Priority	Item	Completed
	Do you need to consider who has access to what credit cards? This can be done in consultation with your partner.	
	Is health insurance still being paid? Who is paying this?	
	Contact school and advise of your situation and ensure child's school has contacts for both parents	
	Consider your privacy. Do you need to change your password or pin number on any bank accounts, email or social media?	
	Do you need to update any legal documents such as wills, power of attorney appointments or enduring guardian?	
	Do you need to make an appointment with your GP or counsellor?	
	Is there anything that is precious to you and cannot be replaced if lost, like a family heirloom or collection? Arrange for their safekeeping.	
	Research and book in for post-separation parenting advice.	
	How much is the mortgage payment? Where does it come from and who is paying this?	
	Make a note of the separation date.	
	Back up your computer or print out or make copies of any important documents.	

These are just a few examples to get you started. You will be able to think of other items that will suit your own unique circumstances.

What information do you have?

Now that we have a list of what we need to do, let's see what information you have and what else you may need. Time to gather all your important documents.

Task 4

Create a list of documents you need to collect. Take a look back at your 'action list'. Do you need any documents to help you complete these items? Let's say on your action list you said you think you need to pay the car insurance or health insurance, but you have no idea when your insurance is due – do you have a copy of the policy? What about the electricity or gas? You may have listed these on your action list. You need to find copies of the bills.

There are also some very important documents you may need down the track. Think about what important documents you have and where they are. Do you have the originals or at least copies of birth certificates and marriage certificates? Do you know what accounts you both have or what superannuation fund you are both with? Do you have copies of the bills you need to pay?

I have created an example list to get you started.

Example document gathering

Item	Completed
Marriage certificate	
Birth certificates	
Passports	
Last three tax returns (personal and business) and notices of assessment	
Most recent payslip	
Details of all bank accounts in joint names, sole name or in any name with any other person and statements for last 12 months	

Item	Completed
Superannuation statements for you both	
Vehicle registration papers	
Vehicle insurance papers	
Title deeds or rates notice for properties	
Details of mortgage and any loan documents	
Copy of any contract for sale of purchase of property	
Home and contents insurance papers	
Loan statements for any personal loans or credit cards	
Copies of any utility bills	
Share statements	
Details of health insurer	
If you have a business or company – make copies of the last profit and loss and tax returns	
Any family trust documents	
Any self-managed superannuation fund documents	
Copies of any current Wills, POA and EG	

Have a look at my list of documents and see if you have or need these documents.

If there is anything you can't find and you think you need it, add that to the bottom of your list and even to your earlier action list. That way, you know that you need to locate this item or ask someone for it.

Tip

If you love organising and planning like me, go through the checklist and create a folder or softcopy of all of your documents so that you can easily locate them when you need them later.

Wrapping it up

By now, you should be feeling calmer. You have set yourself a guide that allows you to follow your very own values, and you know what support is out there to keep you calm.

You should have completed the following tasks:

1. created your personal values list
2. created your own personal behaviour guide
3. started your immediate action checklist
4. gathered the information and documents you require.

Now it's time to move onto step 2, Prepare.

Step 2
Prepare

'By failing to prepare, you are preparing to fail.'

Benjamin Franklin

Prepare emotionally and practically

Preparation is vital. If you are well prepared, you increase your ability to persuade the other side about what you are asking for. You can inform them and educate them of important factors that need to be considered. This gives you both the greatest opportunity to resolve your matter.

Hopefully after working through step 1 you are feeling a little calmer right now. You know exactly how you want to behave, and you have a few helpful lists of things you need to do immediately. You should also have a clear set of values you want to follow, and you have considered and prepared yourself for your behaviour and communication with your ex-spouse.

This second phase is to prepare you not just on a very practical level but also on the emotional level.

Tip

Just because you have finished step 1 does not mean you have to immediately move onto step 2. Sometimes people are just not ready yet to move onto this step. Our emotions are still too high, and we may not have even accepted that the relationship is over yet. So only start this stage when you are ready.

When you are ready …

When you are ready, during this next step I will take you through the types of advice you might need to draw on, why you might need it and where to find it. This means we need to start thinking outside of your immediate needs and start looking a little further forward.

When I talk about emotional preparation, this is going to include (while sticking to those values you have set) looking closely at and thinking about your own needs and goals.

At all times I suggest you keep your set values pinned in your mind (or even on a pinboard or sticky note if you are a visual person) so you can continuously remind yourself how you want to act.

In addition to guiding you through your emotional needs and values, we will start preparing you practically. The reason we do this is so that those emotions do not get the better of you. If you have a clear mind and have good information at hand, you can concentrate on controlling your emotions and ultimately your own path. We need to get rid of any fog, and a lot of the time that simply means getting information and making sure the practical steps are clear in your head.

I will take you through the very practical things you need to think about and prepare to talk about, and help you to consider any other external advice you may need. I find that if you are prepared, although never easy, it is not as difficult. You will have goals to work to and be able to follow a clear and concise path.

Practical preparation

Research

Your advice does not always need to come from an expert. It might be that you are good at researching, or have friends who have had a positive outcome and can provide some good advice. Draw on those things.

If you prefer to research on your own, search for criteria that meet your standards and fit in with your values. I always recommend that instead of searching for legal answers, look at the support that is out there and find people who can talk you through your options. Look for 'out of court options', look for 'alternative pathways'.

Sometimes I have couples who just immediately know what path they want and can stay focused without too much outsourcing. It's time to meet our fourth couple, Monica and Tim. They are a great example of a couple who really knew how they wanted to behave and managed to do a lot of the research themselves.

Couple 4: Monica and Tim (settled on own, used solicitor to prepare)

Monica and Tim have been in a relationship for over three years now. They were never married, nor did they have any children. Monica is a schoolteacher and Tim is a mechanic. Having met when they were in their early 20s, neither had any significant assets and both were just starting out their careers. Monica and Tim were the best of friends, but recently their relationship has been strained as Monica has a real wish to get married and have children, yet Tim really doesn't want to. Despite their best efforts to talk about this and try to move past, Monica has made the very hard decision that she just can't do without these things in her life – they are too important. So, they have made the decision to separate and move on.

Monica and Tim are both very upset by the situation and neither really knows what to do. They really do not want to go to court, and they don't want to spend a lot of money as they really don't have any to spare. At this point they haven't talked about what they want to do, however they are both keen to follow the most peaceful path possible.

Monica does a little research and finds out that she can use the Peaceful Pathway to help her through. She would really like to try to work together through this with Tim; she doesn't see the need for lawyers to help them work it out. She emails the details to Tim and he is more than happy to work through their settlement in this fashion.

Other times couples need more guidance; the best tip I can give you here is not to jump in quickly. Look around for good advice that is consistent with your values. Always make sure you get information about all of your options.

External advice

There are a lot of amazing support services out there, fabulous professionals who are trained to assist separating couples. What do you need to know? Who do you need to talk to? It doesn't just have to be the legal profession; there are accountants, financial planners and family counsellors.

Have a read through each section below and decide if you think that getting this advice in your circumstances would help make things clear. Start creating and preparing your team.

Tip

You can research these professionals now, but you may not always need these professionals this early. It is once again your choice. Just always keep in mind where some extra advice may be helpful.

Family counsellors

I start by mentioning a family counsellor for the reason that, in my experience, not only is it the most used service, but it is also unbelievably valuable. A family counsellor can be used to help you separate, talk to the kids, work on your communication, assist in co-parenting advice … the list is endless.

In addition to looking at a counsellor just for you, a family counsellor or participation in specific separation or communication courses are invaluable. If you haven't needed it initially, you may benefit now.

I have had many clients who were almost unable to talk to each other, and who were so focused on their difficult conversations that they couldn't move forward. I urge you to get this sorted first. Sometimes it takes time to get you and your ex-partner ready to move on. Although you might be seeing a counsellor yourself, a joint session with a family counsellor can assist greatly with moving on and communication; they are also great to help you get your emotions in check and to allow you to be able to focus on solutions.

I recently had a couple who were in the negotiation phase and they were just not getting anywhere. I soon realised that it appeared the reason they were not agreeing was emotional and not practical. They had a few sessions with my family counsellor, and within a few weeks they were both looking at things differently and were able to move forward into their negotiations. I think there was just a lack of communication, a little disrespect, and emotions that were stopping them from being practical. The transformation after the sessions was huge.

Financial planners

Financial planners sit in the same category. They are very useful in negotiations to help work out the best scenario for couples.

If your finances are more complicated than just a house and a car then it may be worthwhile sitting down with a financial planner and getting some really good advice. Again, in a collaborative mediation setting, I use the planner to assist in coming up with solutions that create a positive outcome for both parties using the assets they have together to ensure a secure future ahead.

Accountants

Who totally understands their current financial position? What assets you have, your taxable income, and any taxation obligations? Some do, but there are some who really don't.

An accountant can help here. If you don't have an accountant and you have questions, make an appointment and get some advice.

An accountant is so useful in helping you work out a property settlement. Often, in my collaborative mediation settings I work with the party's accountant, and they help with valuing assets and working out more complicated lists of assets.

Another reason I would suggest you may get advice could be to consider any taxation consequences for selling or transferring assets. Even if you are not sure yet what you are thinking of doing, talk to your accountant so you know what you may need to consider, and have them briefed and ready to help you when you need to call them with any questions.

Brokers and bankers

A broker or banker is someone who can help open some new doors or help you explore some options. Is it one of your goals to stay in the family home? Buy a new home? Not sure? Are you thinking that it might be an option that you sell the family home?

A mortgage broker can help you assess your position and tell you what your lending capacity is. Set up a meeting with your bank or your broker and ask them about this. They will be able to go through this with you based on your budget and monthly income, and establish what amount you may or may not be able to borrow. This is so important. If you have to buy a new home, you really need to know that a bank will actually lend you the money.

Remember, there are always other options. If your bank won't approve you on your own, perhaps you have someone who could assist as a guarantor or provide other security to help you out? Definitely have a talk to your lender or broker to explore all options.

It's time now to meet Frank and Joan. Frank is one of those super-organised personalities who also utilises all his experts to get good advice.

Couple 5: Frank and Joan (Mediation)

Frank and Joan are empty nesters. Frank has just turned 50 and Joan is 48. Their two daughters are in their mid 20s and both moved away a few years ago to attend university, and both now have full-time jobs.

Frank and Joan were married in their 20s. They were set up by a friend, and were married very quickly. Frank is a GP and has his own business in town. He makes a great living, earning about $300,000 per annum. Joan has always worked in the business for Frank and has run the office for him. They have never drawn a wage for her, as they have had enough to survive off the drawings they have for Frank.

Sadly, after the girls left, the relationship between Frank and Joan severely deteriorated. They constantly fought, they weren't enjoying each other's company, and ultimately they sat down together and decided that they would separate. At the moment, they are still living in the house together and this is becoming a real struggle. They are really not sure how to move forward from here.

Joan is really struggling emotionally to deal with the separation, so she has decided to get some assistance from a counsellor. At the same time, she has also made an appointment with a family lawyer who was recommended to her by a friend. Her friend had recently gone through a terrible separation, and told Joan that this lawyer is a real fighter and she should get some advice to make sure that she 'gets everything she is entitled to'. Joan is a little wary, as she really wants to ensure that her relationship stays on a positive path – although she can no longer live with Frank she wants to remain civil for the sake of their daughters. She just wants to sort things out quickly and move out.

Joan has little understanding of their financial position as Frank and their accountant have always handled things. Frank is the organiser when it comes to paying bills, sorting out insurances and so on – she has always left this to him.

Frank makes an appointment with the accountant and asks him to prepare a schedule of assets and liabilities with copies of all relevant documents so that he can give these to Joan to make her feel more informed. Frank also makes an appointment with his broker to seek advice about his ability to borrow; he wants to know how much more he can access to pay Joan out a sum of money.

The key here is to gather all of the required information to prepare both parties practically and to also assist them to look at options.

Finding the right legal advice

I have purposely left the lawyers to last. As you may have already gathered, although I am a lawyer myself, I believe that our role, while vital, is not always required at this step. The best thing we lawyers can do initially is fill your minds with information and options and guide you in the right direction.

Research and advice are often a key element to making sure you can reach a valid, fair and equitable agreement. Make sure you select a lawyer who has a wealth of family law knowledge, who is not litigious, and has your best interests at heart. One who can give you all the options. Why not interview them? Make sure they fit the bill and tick all of your boxes.

You need to make sure you understand what they are saying. They should have an outstanding capacity to communicate with you.

I would also suggest that the virtues of honesty and tough love are important. The lawyer's role is to advise you but also to make sure they are not just telling you what you want to hear.

Tip

You do not have to engage a lawyer yet. The aim is to be informed. Choose them for your team as a backup if you need advice; have them prepared and ready to answer any tricky legal questions you may have and perhaps even to write up or read over any agreement you may reach at the end. You do not have to engage them for the entire process.

Do be realistic about your budget. Ask questions as to costs and timeframes. You will need to make sure you can afford the advice you are asking for. It would be a good idea to even seek a free or initial fixed-price consultation to talk about your concerns. Make sure all options are explained to you, then you can choose when you need to engage a lawyer.

My final tip: find a kind lawyer. I have used this term a few times and I hope you understand it now. There are so many brilliant lawyers out there, and they are amazing litigators. In family law, however, we need to solve a people problem, not just a legal problem. Find a lawyer who is kind and compassionate and who cares about both you and your ex-partner. There are a lot out there.

Let's go back to our first couple: Trish and Marcus. They are my best example of how bad choices – combined with their own terrible behaviour – did not lead them on a peaceful pathway.

Couple 1: Trish and Marcus

So, what do you expect happened after Trish and Marcus both jumped into action and started making drastic changes without communicating?

Well, Marcus immediately called his lawyer. His family had used this lawyer for years and he had meet him a couple of times. He explained the situation and the lawyer immediately took control. He drafted and sent a letter to Trish telling her that she must immediately return the funds and some of the furniture. He also told her that if she didn't, and also didn't produce her disclosure documents to him within 14 days, he would be commencing proceedings against her.

Trish also found a lawyer; she googled 'best family lawyer', and after reading the options, she chooses a large litigation firm that had great reviews and had won numerous awards in the family law area. The lawyer then took over and responded to Marcus's lawyer on her behalf.

After about six months of exceptionally long and nasty letters back and forth, nothing could be resolved. Neither Trish nor Marcus would back down. Marcus was seeking the farm to be transferred to him, and although Trish was happy to do this, she wanted a very large sum in exchange, too large according to Marcus's solicitor.

In the end, Marcus's solicitor commenced proceedings. They were required to first attend mediation but, again, neither party would budge, and they were unable to reach an agreement.

What went wrong here was that neither Trish nor Marcus had researched their options, nor were they explained to them by the lawyers they chose. The outcome when Marcus called his lawyer could have been very different if they had chosen different advisors or sought more information and, of course, behaved themselves.

Knowing your legal options

You really need information about your options. You cannot make good decisions without all of the information first. Research or ask your lawyer what options there are. Do not immediately assume that lawyers and court are the best path. Gather as much knowledge as possible about out-of-court options, mediation and collaborative practice.

Frank is a great example of researching his options.

Couple 5: Frank and Joan

Joan chooses to go see this lawyer. Joan phones the lawyer's office that has been recommended to her. When she phones, she is scheduled in for a one-hour consultation. She is advised in advance that the cost of the consultation and advice will be $495.

The day of the appointment, Joan is very nervous. She really doesn't know what to ask or what she needs to bring, and she is feeling a lot of stress and anxiety. The appointment goes for an hour. The lawyer asks her a lot of questions about her finances, her contributions to the marriage and much more. Joan is totally exhausted by it all, and in fact when she leaves she has a great deal more questions to have answered. She really couldn't answer a lot of the questions that were asked of her; she has little understanding of their financial position and she really has a lot more work to do before she goes much further. She has however chosen to engage the lawyer, and the lawyer has indicated that she will immediately send Frank a letter letting him know that she is acting for her and that she wishes for financial disclosure to be made.

Joan is advised by the lawyer that she will send her a costs agreement that sets out expected costs for each stage of the matter, but also requests an initial $10,000 retainer sum to be placed into her trust account so that she can start working on the matter.

The next week Frank receives a letter from Joan's lawyer explaining to him that Joan has sought her advice and with a very long list of disclosure documents she wants from him, which she refers to as 'financial disclosure'.

At this stage, they are still living together. Frank confronts Joan following the receipt of this letter. He is incredibly angry and confused as to why Joan has so quickly gone and sought advice, and doesn't understand why he is being asked for these documents.

The letter also set out what the lawyer considers to be Joan's contributions to the relationship and what she needs in the future. He said that he was hoping that they could have sat down and talked about this rather than her going straight to a lawyer. He is very disappointed, and the tension between the two gets difficult. He is also highly offended by some of the comments that have been made by the lawyer. This really upsets Joan, as she thought she was just doing the right thing.

They started to yell at each other and things got out of hand. A lot of language was used and comments were made that both really regretted. Neither had any idea what they were to do from here, and both were feeling very lost and confused.

At this step, immediately after a breakup, couples assume that they need to go and get advice or they will be behind. I suggest that it is best (unless there is an urgent or immediate need to get legal advice) to take some time to look at what you need.

If you do choose to go to a lawyer then you can ask that they refrain from sending anything at this point. Just ask for the advice and get the information. If there is no pressing need to start the process now, ask about what other options you have. Can they suggest or explain the mediation process or collaborative law?

After receiving the letter, Frank decides he should go and get his own advice. He is really upset with the manner in which this has happened and wants to try and get things back on track. Despite their separation Frank still really loves Joan and doesn't want to see her going down this path. He knows this is not what she is really like. He researches and finds what is referred to as a 'kind' lawyer. Someone who uses peaceful methods to help resolve family law matters. He likes the sound of this so he phones and makes an appointment.

When he arrives at the initial appointment the lawyer indicates to him that the appointment is to provide information as to his options only, and she is not going to specifically provide any legal advice. Frank is happy with this. She explains to him that there is the option to attend mediation, and if that doesn't work then they can look at other methods such as collaborative practice or lawyer-led mediation or negotiation. She offered that if there were any pressing legal issues or he needed advice on separation circumstances specifically, she could do this, but at this stage she gave him the information he needed to prepare and attend mediation.

When Frank got home, he explained to Joan what he had been told. Joan told Frank that she had no idea that mediation was an option. The lawyer she had spoken to asked her a lot of questions about her relationship and their assets but she didn't explain her options. Joan said that she was very interested in mediation and asked Frank to arrange it.

The key here was Frank finding a lawyer who didn't immediately give legal advice and take legal action; he was told what all the options were first and this was of great assistance.

Preparing emotionally

I find that once you have considered and started accessing any outside advice you may need you will start to feel you are making progress, and you will feel calmer and more in control. Now is the time to start getting a little more emotionally prepared.

What are your needs?

The first thing we need to do is consider what it is that you need. I ask you to remove 'wants' at the moment, as they will tend to confuse your answers. We are just talking *needs* here. The things you need to survive, thrive and move forward.

In any negotiation, setting out very clearly your needs and identifying what issues you have will place you in the best possible position to find solutions. It will assist you to reality-test your approach when you get to looking at options to make sure that any solutions are meeting those needs and interests.

You should consider your needs from a financial, relationships and practical level. It may be that you currently have short-term and long-term interests that are not necessarily the same. You can separate these into interim and long-term interests.

Financial needs

Firstly, let us consider what your financial issues may be on an interim basis. What is your current living situation? Are you living in the house that you and your ex-spouse own? If so, who is paying the mortgage? If it is you, do you still have enough money to cover the payment each month? Where is your day-to-day income coming from now? Do you have a job or are you needing support from your ex-spouse? Who is paying the utilities that were once shared?

If we were considering your longer-term goals, we would be looking more at your housing needs. Are you intending to try to stay in the house and pay the mortgage on your own? Do you have enough income to cover your weekly expenses?

Family needs

What are your family relationship issues, your family's needs? Where are you staying? Where are the kids staying? Are they spending time with the other parent, and if so, when and how does this work? Do you need to make any changes?

Practical needs

What about your practical needs? Do you have a car? What about enough car seats? Can you afford the registration and maintenance of a vehicle? Do you need to talk to the children's school teachers or day-care to advise them of what is happening? If you are moving out do you need new furniture or can you divide some of these things?

* * *

Below is a table showing some of the considerations I find clients have to deal with at this step. It should help you think about these things both on an interim basis and also a longer-term basis.

Task 5

Create a list of needs and issues. Look at all aspects of your current situation. I have provided some examples for you.

Interim needs

- How much income do I have available to me?
- Who is going to pay the mortgage?
- Do I know what all of our monthly expenses and bills are?
- Do I need extra income or child support from my ex-spouse?
- What are our current liabilities and when are the monthly payments due?
- Where will the kids be living?
- How often will the kids spend time with me and with the other party?
- Where will I live? Am I going to stay in the house or get a rental?

Long-term needs

- Can I afford a home loan?
- Can I afford to support myself and the kids on my income?
- Where would I like to live?
- What school will the kids attend?

What are your wants?

Let's now also consider your goals and desired outcomes. You can now start to consider those 'wants' – which are really goals – that keep popping to mind.

The best way to do this at this step is to break that down into two sections. Let's look at your goals for the next six months and then your goals for five years' time.

Whenever you are in a negotiation setting, it's always best to have a goal that you are aiming for so that you know what you can and what you cannot compromise on. It gives you a longer-term vision, and also gives you the short-term motivation to work towards those goals. It will also give you a huge sense of satisfaction when you do get to the point where you have achieved those goals.

Similar to when you are looking at the needs that you have, I am not only going to get you to do this task for yourself, but I want you to consider these goals in light of your family and think about what your ex-spouse may set as goals.

Monica went through this thought process. Let's see what happened.

Couple 4: Monica and Tim

Monica begins work on the preparation stage. Their finances are very simple; they own a house and have a joint mortgage. They have been paying off the mortgage together.

Monica does not want to stay in the house for both personal and financial reasons. She would like a clean start, and feels that there are too many memories in the house. She has looked at her monthly budget and she is also concerned that she wouldn't be able to meet the mortgage payments on her own. She would really like to still be able to buy a house, but something smaller and with a lower mortgage.

She is hopeful that Tim will either want to take over the mortgage or otherwise would agree to sell the house.

She has clearly looked at the issues she needs to solve and worked her goals into the situation.

Create a list of goals

Consider the following in the next six months:

1. What are the five most important things you want to achieve over the next six months? These can be financial goals, lifestyle or even relationship.
2. I then want you to write down why those goals are important to you or your family.

3. Then do steps one and two again standing in the shoes of your ex-spouse.
4. Finally, do steps one to three again for five years' time.

Here are a few examples of each to help you along.

Interim goals

- To maintain a good relationship with my ex-spouse by avoiding arguments and remaining kind and calm.
- To ensure that the kids are seeing both of us regularly.
- I need to make sure that I have enough money at the moment to pay my bills.
- Will I be able to stay in the house until we have sorted out a property settlement? If so, who will pay the mortgage?

Long-term goals

- Maintain a good relationship but sort out our finances.
- I would like to keep the house.
- I would like the kids to stay in the same school.
- I would like to ensure that I have a stable income to cover my week-to-week expenses.
- I would like my children to continue to play their sport.

Task 6

Use the table below to start setting out your short-term and long-term goals. You can keep adding to this as you continue along the pathway. You can change it as you go if you need to. I suggest you think about why each item is important to you; this will help you think through what the most important goals are and perhaps find the ones that really aren't so important and can be compromised on more.

6 months	Why this is important
Your goals	
1.	
2.	
3.	
4.	
5.	
Spouse goals	
1.	
2.	
3.	
4.	
5.	

5 years	Why this is important
Your goals	
1.	
2.	
3.	
4.	
5.	
Spouse goals	
1.	
2.	
3.	
4.	
5.	

You might be wondering why I am asking you to consider what the goals of your spouse may be. Well, I am all about preparing you. You cannot survive in the dark and ignore what goals or options you think your ex-spouse may have. What happens if they are exactly the same as yours? You need to consider what this might mean. Considering what your ex-partner's goals may be will also help you find the peaceful path, because you will be better able to understand where the other person is coming from.

Perhaps one of your goals is to stay in the former matrimonial home and take over the mortgage. That could very well be his or her goal also? You would then need to consider any possible alternatives, and what that means for you both. It's all about being prepared and considering your problem from a very personal angle.

Finalising your personal preparation

I often find that once the right team is created and you have your own goals and needs set out, you will feel comfortable and ready to move onto the next step. The length of time that you remain in this phase, or any phase for that matter, it entirely up to you. Some people may move through this very quickly, others may go slower. That is perfectly fine.

Step 3
Gather

'Information is the resolution of uncertainty.'

Claude Shannon

The process of gathering requires you to bring everything together. To collect as much information from as many different sources as possible. If you can do this stage well then you will be placing yourself in a perfect position to move forward and negotiate. You will have clarity and full transparency about your circumstances and those of your ex-spouse.

After moving through the first two stages, the time has now come to be highly practical and gather all the information you are going to need so you are prepared for the path that lies ahead. This is a very valuable stage as it is useful and essential in all pathways.

If you are choosing to still go ahead alone then you will need to ensure you have all the right information and evidence in front of you so you can accurately discuss your options. The same rule applies if you are choosing to mediate or work collaboratively; you will need to be prepared and have all the required information and documents.

Regardless of the path you are choosing, I will help you gather all the information that allows you to move forward so you can discuss and create your own solutions. This stage will equip you with all of the practical information and tools you need. You simply cannot negotiate well if you are not prepared. Preparation is the key to any good negotiation.

By the end of this stage you will have created your own budget, discovered what information and documents you need, and worked out how to value your assets so that you can prepare a draft list of assets and liabilities and then compare this to your list of needs and wants. This will completely prepare you to enter the exploration phase of the pathway.

Sounds simple? Well, in my experience often the biggest cause of confusion are these very things. So, it is time to get practical for a while.

I will take you through step by step what you need to know and where to find it.

Create a monthly budget

Create a monthly budget. Sounds easy? Well, truthfully, I have come across so many individuals who have no idea what their budget is or who are confused about what they need to include.

It may be that they have left the other spouse to sort out their finances and pay all their bills, or maybe just that they live week to week and pay things as they arise. They never had the need for a budget before.

The key to having a good discussion about money and property is knowing what you need to survive. So, let's budget.

How do you work out your budget?

I am going to show you the simplest of budgets. I am not a financial planner nor an accountant, so this is just a very simple exercise to help you get started and prepared.

If you already have a budget then you really do not need to complete this step; just review and update your budget based on your current circumstances.

If you are someone who needs more help – it may be that your finances are more complicated and you need to seek professional assistance – then by all means you can do this. Go and see your accountant or financial planner and get them to assist you.

For those of you who want to give it a go alone, you can use a budget tool. There are some great ones to be found online, such as at www.moneysmart.gov.au or www.money.com.au. Many banks also have budget tools on their websites, however I have created and use a very simple one that my clients find valuable and tend to use as it is very easy to complete and straightforward.

Tip

Before we start, have your list of issues handy that you created in step 2. You may need to add to this if you are missing something or needing to research some information. You can use my budget tool to help you ensure that you have listed all income and expenses and have an accurate reflection of what you need.

Task 7

Create a budget. Use an online tool or follow along with my example. I will start with a blank budget so you can follow along and insert your own expenses as you go.

Personal monthly budget

INCOME	Value
Income	
Additional Income	
Total Income	
EXPENSES	Value
Housing	
Mortgage or Rent	
Electricity	
Gas	
Water and Sewer	
Phone	
Entertainment	
TV Entertainment	
General Entertainment	
Food	
Groceries	
Dining Out	
Household Cleaning Expenses	
Health	
Health Insurance	
Medical and Dental Expenses	
Vehicle	
Vehicle Payment	
Insurance	
Registration	
Fuel	
Maintenance	
Other	
Total Expenses	
TOTAL	Value
Total Income	
Total Expenses	
Balance	

As you can see, I have broken this down into sections below.

Actual monthly income

This is the money that you earn. It can be from one source or a number of sources. Perhaps it is your wages and or any Centrelink income.

The budget I use looks at your monthly net income. This is the amount that you actually receive in the bank after tax. So, if I was earning $800 net per week then I would insert $800 × 4 = $3200.

If you are not currently working and are receiving Centrelink or Child Support, then insert that here. Also consider that although you may be working you may now be entitled to Centrelink benefits, perhaps a new single parent pension or family tax benefits. Let's say for the purpose of this exercise you get $120 per fortnight. Insert $240 per month. This can be added as extra income.

The total income would then be $3440 per month.

> **Tip**
>
> If you are not sure if you are entitled to benefits, add this to your to-do list. Go and find out what, if any, entitlements you may now have access to with changed circumstances.

Housing expenses

You need to look at all the expenses you have for your home. The main one will obviously be your rent or mortgage. Most people will calculate rent on a weekly basis but a mortgage on a monthly basis; just make sure you are consistent and insert a monthly amount.

Let's say you have rent of $250 per week. Then, in the 'mortgage or rent' row, insert $1000.

You then need to look at the utilities for the house. These include all things that you pay monthly to keep your household running. Your phone, electricity, gas, Foxtel or Netflix, and any council charges such as rates.

If you don't know where to find all this information, this may be one of those questions you need to ask your spouse. I have had couples where one person handled all of the bill payments so the other had no idea what phone or electricity company they were with. Add this to your list.

You will need a copy of the last bill so that you can work out an average monthly cost for these items. If you are unable to find an old statement, you can simply call the company and ask them to email you one or provide the details over the phone. At the very least, you could also look at your last bank statement to see what the monthly debits are.

This method will certainly help for things such as phone, Foxtel and Netflix, but maybe not so much for rates, electricity and gas.

When it comes to items such as rates or water, if you don't have a recent copy of your rates or water notice, phone the local council and ask them to send you a copy. They can also assist you in working out what your annual rates are.

Vehicle costs

Vehicle payment

If you have a car then you are going to need to include expenses to cover it. You will need to find out what finance, if any, is over the vehicle. Is it a lease or private loan? If you are not sure, this may be one item you need to add to the list of issues to ask about or gather more information.

Most vehicles' leases and loans are also paid monthly, so at this stage even if you are unsure as to what type of finance is over the vehicle you should be able to look at your bank statement to find out what the monthly payment is.

Registration and insurance

You will also be likely to have insurance on the vehicle. So again, find out who the vehicle is insured with and insert the amount that you are paying on a monthly basis.

Your licence fee and registrations should also be inserted at this point. This will be an annual fee and you can then divide it by 12 to get your monthly budget amount. Don't forget to include the cost of third-party insurance. For example, my vehicle costs $830 per annum to register and the third-party insurance is $450. So, the total cost to register my vehicle is $1280 or $106 per month.

Fuel

We must not forget fuel. We all use it so put it in there. The best way I have found to do this is to look at your bank statement for the last three months and find out how many times you have purchased fuel. Over three months, I had one transaction per week, so I had filled my car 12 times. I added those amounts up and it was $1260 worth of fuel over three months. I then took the weekly average, so divided it by the three, for the monthly figure and worked out that my monthly average fuel usage is $420.

Maintenance

Even though you do not need to maintain your car every month, you still should put an amount in. I did the same exercise as I did with fuel. I looked at the last 12 months of service costs and maintenance and calculated a monthly figure. I actually had my car serviced twice and paid for tyres. This was $1250 in 12 months, so $104 per month is what I need to insert.

Other items

I have just gone through the essential items here, and if you look at your spending habits you may find that there are many other items that need to go in as they are regular expenses you have. Spend a bit of time here as it is really important to be able to see how much income you have and how much money you need to spend each month.

When we get to the negotiation phase it is likely you will come back to this tool so that you can see if your proposals will work out and fit into your budget.

Take a look at the example I have created. I have $3440 of income and my expenses are $3410. This means that I only have $30 left over a month. I have little room to move when it comes to my living expenses. So when considering outcomes, I need to make sure they are still within this budget.

Personal monthly budget

INCOME	Value
Income	3,200
Additional Income	240
Total Income	**3,440**
EXPENSES	**Value**
Housing	
Mortgage or Rent	1,000
Electricity	60
Gas	80
Water and Sewer	20
Phone	80
Entertainment	
TV Entertainment	50
General Entertainment	
Food	
Groceries	1,000
Dining Out	200
Household Cleaning Expenses	
Health	
Health Insurance	
Medical and Dental Expenses	40
Vehicle	
Vehicle Payment	250
Insurance	106
Registration	
Fuel	420
Maintenance	104
Other	
Total Expenses	**3,410**
TOTAL	**Value**
Total Income	3,440
Total Expenses	3,410
Balance	**30**

Creating a list of assets and liabilities

What are assets and liabilities?

Your assets are the items that you own, your property, your vehicles, money in bank accounts, shares, or your business. They can be in your sole name, in joint names with your spouse, or perhaps with someone else.

If in doubt, list an item and you can review it later. It is better to have an item listed and then decide if it is really an asset that needs to be dealt with rather than ignore it.

Your liabilities are the debts you have. It may be your mortgage, a personal loan, a family debt, or a car loan. Your credit cards or store cards. Anywhere you own money and need to pay it back.

The biggest question and concern for most people is, what do I need to list and what value do I put to it? Couples are often confused as to what is relevant and what they need to list here and, more importantly, how they figure out what the value is.

Let's take a look.

Starting your list of assets and liabilities

Task 8

Start creating a list of assets and liabilities. Use the blank list following and work through the next section to decide what you need to include.

The first step is to start creating a list of what you have. Later in this step you will be gathering all the documents you need, which will hopefully help you add to or clarify some items.

The biggest cause of confusion often is furniture and smaller possessions. Do we list them and give them a value or not? My standard answer is that if they are of significant value, then yes.

Summary of assets and liabilities

Asset	Ownership			Value
	Party A	Party B	Joint	
Bank accounts				
Matrimonial home				
Furniture				
Shares				
Motor vehicle 1				
Motor vehicle 2				
			Total asset pool	$

Liability	Ownership			Value
	Party A	Party B	Joint	
Matrimonial home				
Furniture				
Shares				
Motor vehicle 1				
Motor vehicle 2				
			Total liabilities	$

Net assets $

Superannuation	Fund name	Value	
		At cohabitation	Present
Party A's account			
Party B's account			
	Total superannuation	**$**	**$**

Let's take a look at some of the items you might include in this table.

Jewellery

If you have everyday jewellery like I do, things that mean a lot to you but may not be expensive, you do not necessarily have to list these items. You may want to consider ensuring they are listed just so that you can make sure you retain them, but generally unless they are big-ticket items there is no need to list them in the schedule with a value.

If they are of value, it may be that you already have an appraisal on the items for your insurance – you can use that. If not, you can always go into your local jeweller and obtain a valuation. They will give you a certificate that you can then use to determine the value.

Furniture and household items

I always recommend that people insert something here, but you need to remember that this is not insured value. If you have household contents insurance cover for $100,000, this does not mean that you should use that value.

The method we use is more like the 'garage sale' value. If you were to put all your household items out on the lawn and have a sale, how much would you get? Not many people would achieve more than $5000 for their entire house. I think if you are reasonable here, and don't go over the top, most couples are able to reach an agreed value to use for their negotiations.

I do not recommend you list every item in your house such as toasters, kettles, microwaves, cutlery and crockery. Although they are important to divide or replace, they are not usually of significant value.

Antiques

If you have any antique or big-ticket items in the house, I would list these separately. These are likely to be items that have valuations already as you have included them on your insurance, such as an antique piece of furniture, antique books or artwork.

If you don't have them appraised already for insurance purposes, you can still go and do this. I would suggest you go to a registered valuer to get these done so that they can provide you with a certificate.

Tools and equipment

The same rules apply here as to furniture. What would you get for these items if they were put up for sale? This is not a replacement or insured valued. It's a good idea to list all of your tools as some couples have some really big items here, and then once you have a list you can work out what happens with these items. If any are of greater value they may need to be individually valued.

Again, the majority of couples are also very happy at this step to simply list an agreed total value.

The big-ticket items

Bank accounts and loans

Starting quite simply, look at the current balance of each account you have, and this is the value. You can simply look at the most recent statement, or if you have internet banking, insert the value today.

It could be with a mainstream banking institution or a credit union. It could be a savings account, a term deposit, or an offset account. This doesn't just include accounts you have in your sole name; this also includes any accounts you may have jointly with other persons – your ex-partner, brother, sister, parents.

You should *not* be looking at putting in the value that the account was at the time of separation. We need to know what it is right now. Again, this will be forever changing and can be updated as necessary.

The same goes for any loan accounts; insert the value that is on the current statement or online statement.

Real estate

This is the real property you own. It may be a house, land, a farm or a unit – include any real estate you may have. Again, this can be anything that is in your sole name or joint names with any other person.

Once you have identified your real estate it is then time to work out what it is all worth. There are a few options here. If you are considering selling the house then I would suggest you obtain three market appraisals so that you know what the sale range may be if you do go ahead with that option.

If you are wanting to look at the option of keeping the property or your ex-spouse may want to keep it, then I would suggest you organise a registered valuer. Now this will cost you. In my region they can cost anywhere from $600 to $1000, but depending on the type of property, perhaps it is rural, I have seen the costs being higher.

One thing to consider at this point is what we call a 'joint valuation'. This is when both you and your ex-spouse consider getting this valuation done jointly and agree to negotiate on that value. So, do consider holding off on paying for your own individual valuation if you think this might be something you can talk about when you get together to discuss your settlement.

At this point, you may look at just getting appraisals, so you have a general idea of price range. You can approach your local real estate agent and they are usually very happy to come and have a look at your property and give you an appraisal. Sometimes it benefits to get more than one so that you have a good idea of the price range.

You will also need to know the current debt that is secured over the property, if any. Check out your latest statement online or your last loan statement to get a recent value.

Vehicles

You should have the details from your registration papers that will assist you in obtaining an estimate of the value. The most used method is Redbook (www.redbook.com.au) which allows you to insert the make, model and year to obtain a price guide. You can go one step further and purchase a valuation report, which will take into account the kilometres and condition. The cost of each vehicle at the time of writing is $33 including GST.

It is then important to work out what you currently owe. It may be as simple as looking at your most recent loan statement, or if you have a lease then you can call your leasing company and ask them to provide you with a current payout figure. Yes, once again, this will change as time passes, so you may need to obtain updated payout figures, but for the purpose of this exercise, you need to get the current payout figure.

Monica and Tim completed this task well.

Couple 4: Monica and Tim

Monica works on gathering all the relevant information. She makes arrangements for three agents to value the house and then she takes an average of the values. She believes the house is likely to be worth $400,000 based on the average of these three appraisals. She checks her online banking and confirms that the current joint mortgage is $200,000.

She has a Honda Civic and Tim has a Nissan Navara. She inserts all the details into Redbook, and she can see that the Honda is only likely to be worth $10,000 and the Nissan is the same.

She inserts all of her assets and liabilities into a schedule of assets and liabilities so that she can clearly see what the total their assets are worth.

She suggests Tim talk to their bank, then they could sit down together and see what he can afford. After Tim has spoken to the bank they decide to sit down and review everything. Monica brings the schedule of assets and liabilities and they go through this together. Tim agrees with the values that Monica has attributed to each of the items. They can determine that their joint net worth is $220,000.

Other items

Once again, I am just focusing on the most common items that you are likely to have. If you have an interest in a trust, business or company, it might be best to talk to your accountant who can assist you in valuing or obtaining a formal valuation of these items.

Finalising the list

It may be that you need some more information before you can finalise your list. That is okay; the next step will set you up to help with this. It may also be that you need to wait to talk to your spouse as you need more information. That is okay too. This is just to get the process started.

Gather your documents

Time for a little harder work. This task itself can be a little daunting, but once done, you will save yourself so much time and money in the future. This is definitely a step you can get ready and organise personally; you do not need to pay someone to do this for you.

This section is a basic guide to show you what the most common documents you *need* will be, and where to find them. And more importantly, what you will then do with them once you have them.

Why do I need to gather my documents?

In Australia, you have an obligation to make sure you disclose all assets that you each have, whether it be in your sole name, joint names or in any other structure.

If you do not list items or fail to disclose them, this can be later seen as fraud if you have signed a declaration to say what your assets are. You can certainly obtain legal advice on this, but for the purpose of this negotiation pathway, you need to make sure you have everything covered so the result you come up with is acceptable.

In addition to this being a requirement for legal reasons, it is also a requirement in my process for moral reasons. How can one negotiate and agree on a settlement if they aren't really sure what the assets are, who owns what and how much it is worth? It would be totally unfair to expect someone to agree to a settlement when they are in the dark as to what they are agreeing to give up or get.

Finally, gathering your documents and having them handy will assist you with the valuation phase of this step.

What documents do I need?

I am going to keep it very simple and will just deal with the items most of my clients commonly have or have difficulties with. You may have more or less, but in any event this step requires you to take a good look at what you actually own, what debts you have and what evidence you have of all of these things.

The best way to start this process is to use the list of assets and liabilities you have just created. The documents you require will vary from asset to asset; the more information you can gather the better. I will go through some standard assets and liabilities that you may have to help you identify the documents you might need to locate.

Task 9

Start collecting all the documents that you will need for your negotiations.

Bank statements

Let's start simple. What you would have done so far is list all bank accounts you have and what the current balance is.

You should obtain at least 12 months' worth of statements for each of those accounts. The easiest way to access this is simply via your online banking. If you have numerous accounts, you can use some awesome software that automatically collates your statements. (Check out my tips below on this.)

You should do this process not only for investment and savings accounts but also for loan accounts and credit cards you have with any bank or financial institution.

Real estate details

You need to list the address and the title description (your lot and deposited plan number). The best place to find this is on your rates notice. On your rates notice you will find your title reference details. This is usually a lot number and a plan number, and is listed under or next to the address. Repeat this for every item of real estate you own.

The reason I suggest you get a copy of your rates notice within your documents is that it usually contains a lot of relevant information you may need for discussions with a lawyer, writing your agreement or for a valuer.

Some other documents that may be useful (but not absolutely necessary) to get hold of at this stage for your real estate interests are:

- a copy of your home insurance
- 12 months of loan statements
- a copy of your original loan documents
- a copy of the original contract for sale when you purchased the property.

These documents can be used to clarify things when discussing how much the house has increased in value since you purchased and how much has been paid off any loans.

Vehicles and finance documents

Most people will simply have a motor vehicle; however, consider here too that if you have motorbikes, trucks or even trailers or boats they can go into this section. You will be best to locate your registration papers. If you cannot find them you can go to the relevant roads and vehicles service in your state and request copies.

Secondly, do you have a loan over a vehicle? If so, then what type of finance is it? If you can get hold of your original loan documents, you will be able to identify this. It may be that you simply have a car loan, or you may have something more complicated like a novated lease. Whatever it is, at the very least, obtain a copy of the relevant document you signed when purchasing the vehicle so that you can identify this information.

The documents you need to gather here are:

- a copy of your registration papers
- third-party and any comprehensive insurance
- 12 months of loan statements
- any loan or lease documents over the vehicles.

Business details

If you have an interest in a business or a company, you need to obtain the documents that are relevant to this. The first thing you need to know is the structure of the business: is it a sole trader, partnership or company?

Regardless of the business structure, you should obtain copies of the last three tax returns and your current Profit and Loss and Balance Sheets. You should also gather any of the abovementioned documents that are relevant to your business such as bank statements, vehicle registrations and loan agreements.

This may be a stage where you need some extra advice if you have a complicated structure. So check out my advice below about this.

Share Holding information

This one is relatively easy in most cases; you will need to obtain a copy of your share statement. If you cannot locate these share statements then you can contact the relevant company directly and their share department should be able to get the information for you. Another simple method might be to check your last tax return, as you are likely to have disclosed income from dividends. If in doubt, contact an expert such as your accountant or financial planner and they can assist you.

You can ascertain the most recent value by looking at the current value on the stock market or contacting your broker.

Superannuation details

I find that a lot of clients have accounts with more than one superannuation company as they have worked a few jobs. If this is the case, you will need to obtain the most recent statement for each one. This can be done by logging into your account online or by phoning the superannuation company directly.

If you have a MyGov account then you should also be able to see your superannuation interests there. You will still however need to obtain a statement directly from the company.

Income details

You will also need to ensure you have the correct documents to clarify and verify your income. Payslips and benefits statements are best used here, as well as producing the last three income tax returns and notices of assessment.

Other documents

There will be many other types of assets I have not included here, as I have just selected a few of the most common ones to help get you started. The main thing to remember is to identify each asset and then locate any documents you have that are relevant to that item.

Tools to help you gather your documents

I have come across many different personalities; some love the exercise of gathering documents, and usually they are the ones who already have the perfect folder sitting on their shelf with every item neatly copied and labelled with a tag, and they can go and get this information within a few minutes.

Then I have the clients who have absolutely no idea, and they simply throw away statements or documents when they arrive or throw them into a pile to read later.

If you are one of those chaotic-style personalities, here are a few tips for you. Or even if you are a spreadsheet enthusiast, you may even love this more than your current system.

Take a look at Adieu (www.adieu.ai). This is a very clever tool designed by an accountant who was constantly getting requests from separated couples to produce their financial information to their solicitor. Not only is this time consuming, it costs money.

He has designed a program that will do it for you. At the time of writing this book, the fee is $300. What it does is allow you to upload all your relevant documents into a dashboard. You use a one-time password for your bank accounts, and it will upload the statements for you. You do not need to log into and upload all your individual statements from each bank. I just love this! It will also allow you to access other sites such as the ATO to download your tax returns and superannuation information.

Finally, it allows you to upload any other documents you may have. So, if you have your rates notice, valuation or rego papers, you can upload them here and keep everything in the one place! You can also then share it with others if you need to.

It is available for lawyers to use on your behalf, but is also accessible directly for couples. I get super excited about this!

I use Family Property (www.familyproperty.com.au). As a lawyer and mediator, and yes serial organiser, I just love looking at ways to organise information and make it easier for clients to share information.

Now at the time of writing I believe it is only available to lawyers and mediators, but, depending on what path you take, this may be a useful option that is used by them too, so worth a look. It has similarities to other AI document systems where you can upload your documents and it will assist with gathering bank statements directly from the bank and also allow you to upload other documents, and it also has many other added benefits. It allows your lawyer or mediator to enter and play with proposals and outcomes, great to use later in the process when looking at options and outcomes.

Finally, to help you out, below is my own checklist that my clients use to review what documents they need to gather. It is not fully comprehensive, but is a guideline that is used by my clients. You may have more documents to collect depending on your assets and liabilities, or you may have fewer.

Document checklist

- [ ] 12 months of bank statements for all bank accounts
- [ ] 12 months of credit card or loan statements for all accounts
- [ ] Rates notice for all properties
- [ ] Any property valuation or appraisal you may have
- [ ] Home and contents insurance
- [ ] Home loan documents
- [ ] Original contract for when you purchased your home
- [ ] Vehicle registration papers
- [ ] Third-party and/comprehensive insurance papers
- [ ] Vehicle finance documentation
- [ ] Vehicle loan statements for 12 months
- [ ] Business/company tax returns and notice of assessment for last three years
- [ ] Business/company profit and loss and current balance sheet
- [ ] Current superannuation statements for all superannuation interests
- [ ] Share statements
- [ ] Last three payslips and/or benefit statements
- [ ] Individual tax returns and notices of assessment for last three years

What other information might you need from your partner to negotiate?

It may be that you simply don't have access to some information, and you need this from your partner. That is okay; they too have a positive obligation to disclose and therefore need to provide you with any information you need. So, jot that one down on your action list to make sure you request a copy of such information from them.

I want to come back to Jennifer and William, who last time we looked at them had decided they would be going ahead with their separation.

Couple 2: Jennifer and William

Jennifer starts the process of reviewing their financial situation and makes her lists with regard to their assets and liabilities and what she thinks might work. She also prepares a budget for each of them. She soon realises that it would be unlikely that either of them would be able to maintain a mortgage on their own.

She decides to go and seek some assistance from a lawyer. She chooses what she believes to be a kind and calm lawyer, who her brother referred her to. He had separated just recently and spoke very highly of the lawyer. He explained that he kept things very calm and gave him lots of great advice about out-of-court solutions.

After her appointment she is feeling much better. The lawyer gave her some really great advice about her options and what she needed to do from here. After the appointment, Jennifer felt she had enough information to get prepared and hopefully be able to sit down with William herself.

Jennifer had been informed by the lawyer what information she needed to gather before she could start negotiating with William. She decided to use Adeiu, and at the cost of $300 she was able to enter a onetime passcode for her various bank accounts and all of her bank statements were automatically uploaded. She was also then able to obtain her tax returns in the same way. She collected all of her other documents and uploaded them to the same dashboard. She also had a very clear picture of the total value of their assets and liabilities.

Her result was a very clear picture of all of her assets, and she had all the corresponding paperwork to move onto the next step.

Bringing it all together

Right now, you should have a budget, a schedule of assets and liabilities, and have started gathering all of your documents. This is a huge achievement.

These items are essential, whether you choose to negotiate alone, if you go to mediation or use a lawyer. The benefit here is that you have everything available and you have a great idea of what things are worth, and this in itself will save you a lot of time and money.

The next part of the book will take you through the task of comparing your needs and interests, looking at the assets you have, and trying to come up with a few solutions so that you can be prepared to enter into discussions.

Step 4
Explore

'We shall not cease from exploration, and the end of all our exploring will be to arrive where we started and know that place for the first time.'

TS Eliot

After completing all the hard preparation work, we now need to start working through and assisting you to explore your options, your needs, and how those might fit into your unique circumstances.

At step 2 we started exploring what issues and needs you have. We looked at financial issues, family issues and practical needs. One of your tasks (task 5) was to create a list. The list at that stage was to assist you in ensuring that you were immediately prepared, you knew what information you needed, and what might have been missing.

This stage takes you a little further. You can start thinking about what your primary interests are in this journey and possibly some ways to achieve your long-term goals.

What does the exploration phase involve?

Exploration is all about discovering new things, new places and different experiences. The same theory applies when creating your Peaceful Pathway; we are going to be breaking new ground, walking on some fresh grass. During this stage of your journey it's so very important to be open minded and really push yourself to consider new options, alternative options, even options that may not seem perfect. Then, you will walk through, test and explore all of these possible avenues.

The beauty of exploring and testing yourself at this stage is that when you are ready to discuss and negotiate, you can demonstrate that you have carefully considered all options. It is no good coming up with some great plan if it is never going to work out for you or is completely unachievable. You can explore the pros and cons of each option and, hopefully, between the two of you, create some really great solutions.

One lesson I learnt in running mediations as a lawyer is that things are not always as I see them. I have had couples come to me, I take them through an intake, and before we even reach the joint discussion stage I feel I have a clear idea in my mind as to how this can be resolved.

I found I was often wrong.

So, I have had to learn to sit back and let couples create their own solutions – very hard after 15 years of being a lawyer who tells clients their best option. Then, to my surprise, while exploring, together they would come up with a plan that I hadn't even considered. They joined together to review their ideas, needs and interests, and create a perfect pathway for them. This is what I call the Perfect Peaceful Pathway, and it is wonderful to see it develop.

The key to a good exploration

Have you ever tried to walk in someone else's shoes? Not literally, but metaphorically. Have you ever truly sat there and thought about what it would be like to be them?

The key I have found to letting this happen is careful consideration of your ex-spouse and trying to think like them, trying to see what they feel and need. You did this in the goals section.

So again, not only do you need to think about what *you* might need and what your main interests are, but if you can turn your mind and do the exact same exercise for your spouse then you will have considered more avenues and have a greater chance of coming up with a solution that also suits your ex-spouse.

This section is not about working out what the 'solution' is, it is about coming up with a list of possible outcomes and suggestions that you can review and test with your ex-partner. This will equip you to enter into really comprehensive and fruitful joint discussions.

Tip

Avoid a fixed position. What I want you to avoid is approaching your ideas and ultimately your negotiations with a 'yes or no' attitude. The clients I see fail at negotiation are the ones who have one and only one outcome that they will agree too, a fixed position. Often this is not actually the best solution for them and they end up fighting for the wrong outcome. We need to be flexible and consider all options before you can reach an agreement.

So, open your mind and make sure you consider all aspects, what may or may not work for you, the pros and cons of each scenario, and also what you think your ex-spouse may want and need.

Think win/win

I recently read *The 7 Habits of Highly Effective People* by Stephen R. Covey. His insight and explanation of the six paradigms of human behaviour are spot on for me when it comes to family law negotiations. The win/win frame of mind is the one that seeks a mutual benefit for both parties. It means that the agreements that are reached or solutions created are mutually beneficial to both of the parties. The result is that two people can walk away feeling good about the situation and ultimately are highly committed to what they have created. This is what we should be aiming for; it is a better way to look at things.

He even goes to the extent of explaining the win/win or no deal concept. This means that if an agreement cannot be reached that will mutually benefit both parties, it should not be a made.

I have found that if you can really embrace the exploration phase and look at all avenues, you will be so much closer to finding a solution that is win/win.

What you need to consider now

Every couple is different. I have some couples who simply just want a very even division of their assets, as they started with nothing and both feel they grew their asset pool together, and other couples where they are both very clear that one should get a little more or less due to the history or current circumstances around their relationship. Others have no idea.

Family law in Australia is very much a no-fault system; it's not like the American TV shows and movies where people try to catch their spouse cheating so that they get nothing when they separate. We are very much about fairness and equity.

This book is not about giving legal advice, it is about creating solutions that work for you and your family, avoiding the litigation system and saving your relationship, whatever new form it may take. If at any point you do however feel overwhelmed and need that little extra advice or support, please do go back to my section on choosing the right advice and seek information from a lawyer.

I am a strong believer that creating a family law solution is not about fighting for your 'rights', it is about ensuring you have the right outcome for your family. This might not always follow the path a court would take, and that is okay.

However, you do need to consider these issues on a personal level. You need to be open and realistic about the factors that may affect the outcome and ensure that on a personal or moral level you are okay with the solution.

The reason we do this here is so that there is not any hidden animosity or surprises that might ultimately make your agreement fall over. If we lay it out on the table, talk about it and create a solution with all of the information, we have a much better chance of reaching an agreement and that agreement being finalised.

There are so many things that will affect how you divide your assets, both on a legal and practical level. These include the financial and non-financial influences you have each had on the relationship and, more importantly, your wealth and assets.

What did you both contribute?

Try thinking about what assets you had when you and your ex-spouse commenced your relationship. Then look at what happened during the relationship and what your future financial needs may be. The reason we look at this is we need to ensure that any agreement you reach is fair and reasonable on all levels.

Example 1

If one of the parties (party A) came into the relationship with a house that they had almost paid off (let's say it is valued at $500,000 and they only owe $100,000), party A is bringing in $400,000 worth of equity at the start of the relationship.

The other party (party B) has had a difficult time and is in debt with credit cards of $50,000.

The parties stay together for three years, and then sadly split. They have no children, and have during their relationship both worked and shared the expenses.

Party A has continued to pay off the mortgage and now only owes $50,000, and the house is now valued at $650,000. So at the time of separation, the asset is worth $600,000.

Do you think that party B should be entitled to half of that equity?

Well, after carefully discussing and considering what they did and did not contribute to the relationship and their current wealth, parties A and B decided that party A should get a greater amount out of their current assets.

All I am asking you to do here is consider what your contribution and that of your spouse may have been so that you can discuss this. Again, try putting yourself in the other person's shoes and see how you think you would like your contributions to be treated. There is no benefit in ignoring this.

A close look at contributions

Let's look at this a little closer so that you can consider this carefully:

- **Start of the relationship:**

  Take your mind back to when you first moved in together. What did each of you have? Did you have any significant assets such as a house or savings? List anything important you can think of, and if possible also insert the value of these items. Also now consider what your ex-spouse may have had.

- **During your relationship:**

  The period you then need to look at is the time you were together. Take some time to think about what you have each done financially during the relationship. You can list items such as lump sums from family, perhaps a redundancy or inheritance. You may even feel there were greater non-financial contributions by one party. Maybe you cared for a sick partner or they were travelling a lot, so you had to care for the children and the household alone? Did one of you physically renovate the house yourself?

- **Following separation:**

  This is also important to consider. Sometimes couples don't look at doing a property settlement for some time after separation, even years later. You need to consider what you or your spouse may have done. Did only one of you pay the mortgage? Perhaps you made some renovations to the house? Consider anything that you or your spouse may have done that has added value to the assets you currently have.

What you need to consider moving forward

At this stage you need to consider what the future looks like for you and what you are going to need to survive. Do you have a lower income or illness that will reduce your ability to earn? Does the other party have much greater financial resources that you do? Does one party have the vast majority of care of the children? Consider anything that is going to affect your day-to-day living and ability to meet your financial needs in the future.

Task 10

I want you to go through each of the elements and create a comprehensive list. Consider each item with care, and be practical. Put yourself in your ex-spouse's shoes; would you want to be acknowledged in some way for the things you did?

Things to consider

List of contributions	Date	Estimated value
Start of relationship		

During the relationship		
Following separation		
Future needs		

If you complete this list, it will also assist you in your own discussions, or if you are using a mediator or lawyer to assist you they will have some really good background information to be able to advise you with.

Remember that the benefit of this exercise if not to show that one person did more than the other, or deserves more, but it is to ensure that we are considering on a moral and practical level what you might each need. It is still your choice as to how you separate your property.

Here is another couple of examples to help you:

> Party A and party B had no real assets when they met. During their relationship they had two children who are now aged two and five. They have split after seven years.

During this time, party B received an inheritance from his mother in the sum of $80,000. They decided to place this amount onto their joint mortgage to reduce their debt.

At the time of separation, party A isn't working as she stays at home to care for the children. Party B is earning $120,000 per annum. They only have the house, which is valued at $300,000, and they owe $50,000 plus have a car each – both are of minimal value.

Party A and party B have discussed the contribution that party A made from his mother and also the fact that party A has a greater future financial need as she has little income and cares for the children as party B has a very demanding job. They both agree that the contribution of party B and the needs of party A are similar and decide to divide the equity in their home equally.

Another example:

Party A and party B have been married for 25 years and have two children who are 20 and 22 years of age. When they first got together, they didn't have any assets or liabilities.

During their relationship they both worked full time, except for the period that party A went on maternity leave to care for the children.

All of the assets that they acquired were purchased and paid off together. They are both now in their mid-50s and can work until retirement.

They have decided that it's fair and reasonable to equally share the equity in their assets.

Creating a list of possible outcomes

Tip

This is not about looking at percentages. It is about considering on a human level what you have each contributed and what you need for the future.

Once you have considered your contributions and possible future needs, we can move onto the task of creating some possible outcomes. As a mediator this is one of my favourite stages; it's wonderful to see clients discuss all of their needs and interests and then work together to come up with solutions. Remember, however, that before I sit them in a room together, I have asked them to carefully consider a few possible outcomes. They do all this preparation beforehand.

Creating a list of possible outcomes and solutions is by far one of the hardest tasks for most couples, but if you have done the background work it is easier.

Task 11

Start a list of possible outcomes.

Option	Solution	Benefits or issues with solution
1		
2		
3		

Let's walk through this together; you should have already completed the relevant worksheets so pull them all out so you can go over them – they will help:

1. Go right back and take another look at what you included on your list of morals and values (task 1).
2. Next look at the issues and interests you listed that you have, and those listed for your partner (task 5).

3. Review the goals you are hoping to achieve and those that you think your partner will be seeking (task 6).
4. Pull out your information guides, your budget (task 7) and your list of assets and liabilities (task 8).
5. Finally, consider the list of contributions and future needs that you each have (task 10).

If you have completed all of these tasks you will be well placed to start considering outcomes.

Start a list of possible outcomes

In order to get you thinking, let's look at a simple scenario to help you work through your own:

Step 1: Your values are respect and honestly.

Step 2: Your interests are the stability and security of your children.

Step 3: Your goal is to have a family home.

Step 4: Your assets and liabilities are as follows:

Assets	
Family home	$300,000
Vehicle 1	$20,000
Vehicle 2	$5,000
Bank accounts	$5,000
Total	**$330,000**
Liabilities	
Home loan	$120,000
Credit card	$2,000
Total	$122,000
Net	**$208,000**

Superannuation (H)	$100,000
Superannuation (W)	$20,000
Total	**$120,000**
Net value assets (including super)	$328,000

Step 5: Neither you nor your husband had any assets when you got together. You have two children and have worked part time while your husband has worked full time. You now have a good stable income and your children are at high school and your husband is paying child support. You do not consider there are any differing contributions or financial needs.

Option 1

The first option here is that you would like to try and keep the family home, as this is the home that you feel would create the most stable environment for your children moving forward. You have $328,000 of assets to divide, including super.

Let's exclude super at this point and just look the assets that value $208,000.

If you were to keep the house, you will need to pay out the current joint loan of $120,000 and refinance this into your sole name. You will also need to borrow extra to pay out your ex-spouse. You would like to keep the family car – it will be needed to travel with the kids. You believe that everything should be divided equally. So that means you each get $104,000 in assets and $60,000 in superannuation.

Test: Can this work?

You retain the equity in house	$180,000
Car	$20,000
Credit card	–$2,000
Total	**$198,000**

In this scenario, if you take over the house and the mortgage and keep the car you will have $198,000 worth of assets, $94,000 more than half. Too much.

So, if your husband keeps the cash of $5,000 and the $5,000 vehicle, he will only have $10,000. You would therefore need to pay him $94,000 by way of a cash payment.

This means you would need to borrow $214,000 from the bank in your sole name. That is the $120,000 to refinance the loan into your own name and $94,000 to pay your husband.

Reality test: Go back to your research: what was the maximum amount of your budget and income that the bank will lend you?

Also consider, is this a debt you think you can handle long term? Even if the bank says you can afford it, are you comfortable with the monthly repayments?

Option 2

What if the house was sold and you each received 50% of the sale proceeds. This would mean you would end up with approximately $90,000. There are some small adjustments for the vehicles, but it still leaves you in a position where you could perhaps look for a smaller house, or something more affordable.

Option 3

You ex-spouse takes over the mortgage and pays you out a sum of money. You may not have enough to buy a house, but it is a deposit. You could rent in the meantime until you have saved enough money and settled in your new routine.

Tip

Remember, the scenario I used here is very basic and I really haven't taken you too far with the solution – these are just three very basic options. You may have some more brilliant suggestions that better suit your needs and make things work for you both.

Guides to help create solutions

If you are feeling stuck, go back and use those amazing people that I spoke of earlier. Find a kind lawyer, a savvy accountant or financial planner. I use these options often when trying to look at solutions for my couples. Draw on all the resources you can to create a win/win solution.

If you are keen at trying it alone and are just looking for some assistance, as I mentioned earlier there have been so many advances in this area recently. At https://amica.gov.au they have created a program that will allow you to input your assets and liabilities, and answer questions about your circumstances. The site can then suggest an outcome. Do remember, however, that this type of assistance is more of a 'possible legal outcome' rather than a creative one. I am still a big fan of using people as the powerful tool here.

I am a great believer that if we want to be amicable, follow our morals and values, and consider all of our circumstances then we can create great solutions, whether or not the legal system tells us they are perfect. The choice is still ours to find the Peaceful Pathway.

Step 5
Negotiate

'Negotiation talks are the best way to solve anything. We must replace wars and weapons with negotiations and talks.'

Akbar Ganji

A negotiation is the exercise of having discussions with someone so that you can achieve, arrange, or agree on an outcome. This is not meant to be a fight; this is the chance for you both to sit down together and create a peaceful solution that you can both be happy and proud of. This is the stage where you start working together. You and your ex-spouse will need to both be in a position where you feel you are prepared and ready to talk. Communicate and make sure that you are both happy to move onto this step. At this time you can choose to go it alone and continue with step 5 or you can move straight to my "Other Pathways" section of this book. I really hope you can be in a position to try it yourself.

If you do want to start alone, check in with each other to make sure you have completed all the preparation work. To start a negotiation unprepared sets you up for failure. The key to any negotiation is preparation. You have everything you need now to be able to sit down together to discuss and to be ready to explore all of your options.

Getting started

Before you start, I will give you a few preliminary steps to set you up. You will need to create the right atmosphere to ensure you are both feeling safe and comfortable. Keep that pathway nice and calm.

You will set an agreed agenda. You need to make sure you know exactly what you need to talk about and in what order, and you need to review and agree on the items you are going to be negotiating on. You need to keep on track.

You will work through your list of assets and liabilities together this time.

Then you start the work on achieving an outcome.

The great thing in this stage of the process is that you will utilise a lot of the hard work and preparation that you have already done and bring it all together.

Creating the right atmosphere

Have you ever walked into a room, into a stressful situation, and felt immediately uncomfortable with your surroundings and just wanted to walk straight back out again? I have, and it never went well for me.

I know that if I am feeling uncomfortable and struggling with my surroundings, outside influences and distractions, I just cannot think straight. It is hard to concentrate and make clear decisions.

In a negotiation setting, especially one that you are creating on your own, your surroundings, the space and even the attendees are so important to you feeling comfortable. When I talk atmosphere, I am also talking about creating an environment that makes you both feel safe and secure to talk. I am not suggesting you need to go to any great lengths, just consider the basics.

Location

This is entirely up to you. Some people like a neutral environment, others feel safe and comfortable in the family home. Just make sure you have a quiet and comfortable space where you can sit down and even make yourself a cup of tea or have a coffee if needed.

Timing

You need to make sure you have no other commitments and have ample time for your discussions. When I take my clients through the negotiation process, I will suggest we have several meetings, but generally each discussion should last for no more than two hours, so make sure you have uninterrupted time available.

Try to avoid having too much on that day – no other commitments. You need a clear mind and to not feel you need to rush off to be somewhere else.

Attendees

This discussion needs to be just between the two of you, unless there is a very good reason for someone else to be present, such as a mediator, lawyer or accountant.

I often have clients ask if they can bring in a support person. My first thought is that if they need a support person then they are probably not ready to negotiate. This needs to be a decision that is made on your own with no outside influences.

Recently I had a couple who called me after failed discussions. The wife had asked the husband if she could bring her parents into the discussion to help her. What ended up happening was the parents took over the discussion and (in obvious love and support of their daughter) did all the talking for her, and ultimately they weren't able to reach an agreement on their own and needed my help. I believe that if the husband and wife had been in that room alone they would have had a much greater chance of talking things through and coming up with solutions.

These are not discussions that your kids should be privy to. Do not do this when the kids are around or are within ear shot.

Behaviour

In any mediation setting I have standard rules of behaviour. These can also apply to you. They are quite simple:

1. Do not use any derogative or negative language. Be respectful.
2. Let the other person speak – do not talk over them.
3. Do not raise your voice and yell at the other person. If you are getting upset, take a break.
4. Listen to what the other person is saying.

I know this is not easy, no matter what the circumstances, talking about dividing your assets and making huge life choices. In fact, I would say that it is one of the hardest things that you will do in your life. The point to remember here is that you are prepared; hopefully you have both followed my process and are both on the same page and ready to talk.

The path is of your choosing. If you can act in a manner that is in line with your values and keep remembering them throughout the discussions, you will be well placed. If you choose to get angry and use harsh words then things are likely to head along a negative path.

You can choose your emotional response. Do not follow another's bad behaviour. You can choose your reaction or non-reaction. *You* can choose how you respond and how you engage, and often the other person will follow you.

You are in this negotiation as you want to work through this together and stay amicable, so do that. Think about the end of the pathway and what you want it to look like if you are struggling. If you need a break, take a break.

Finally, remember the most important tip I can give you here is to listen. If you don't listen properly, you may miss an opportunity to understand or create a possible solution.

Task 12

Set up a meeting and create the right atmosphere.

My meeting schedule

Not every situation can be resolved amicably in the one sitting. Actually, I would say very little can be resolved in one sitting. I am suggesting you need a few meetings. I know that I get totally exhausted and drained when running mediations, and my solution now is to split up the agenda into a few different meetings. Do not try to do this all in one sitting.

Have you ever heard of those couples who engage a mediator and are asked to set aside three or four hours to work through the mediation? I am such a huge advocate of mediation, but who can sit there for three or four hours working on finances, creating solutions and end up with a good agreement? The three- or four-hour mediations I have been involved in are more like four to six hours. Totally and utterly exhausting. The longest I ever had was eight hours, and by the end of the day my client was in tears and just said to me: 'I don't care anymore, I will just agree. I can't take it anymore.' It was then that I realised this was not a mediation, it felt more like a battle ground and we were just waiting on one party to retreat.

Now when I mediate, I separate the steps of the process, to create some space. That is exactly how I have been doing it now for the last two years and there is no reason why you can't follow the same path.

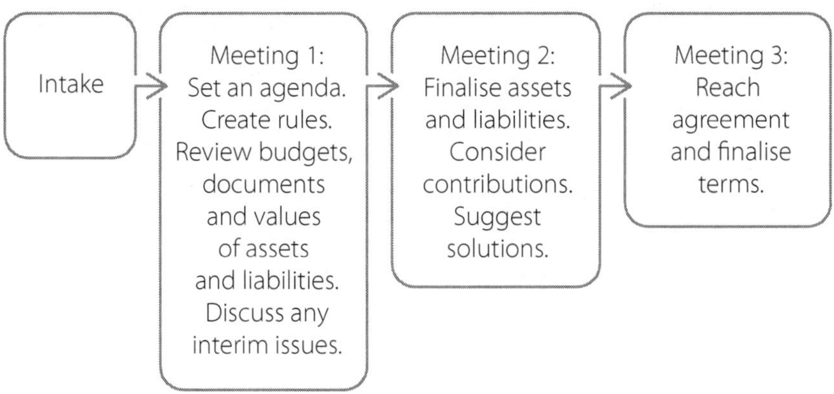

The first meeting

As I do, you can use the first meeting to go through the initial discussions about your assets and liabilities. This is a very practical meeting. We take this opportunity to exchange any documents we have and make sure that we aren't missing anything.

This is also the time to talk about any interim issues you may be experiencing. Perhaps there are issues with mortgage payments, income or insurances. You can raise them here and deal with them together.

Often you will find there is still a little homework to do, some more information to go and get. The break in between meetings gives you a little more time to go over this and get anything else you might realise is needed.

The second meeting

The second meeting is where we come back and finalise the schedule of assets and liabilities after doing any homework, and we confirm and agree on what the total pool of assets is worth. You should have a discussion about what contributions or future needs you think should be considered in the outcome.

We also then start to explore options and each other's financial needs by doing a little reality testing and make sure the solutions are going to work.

Again, sometimes there is a little homework required. You might need to check in with your bank as to your lending capacity, or even just need a little time to think about a few of the options created.

The final meeting

Finally, I have a session where we create the final agreement. We review all the terms of the agreement, how it will work and who will need to do what. There is often so much to think about even after you have that basic agreement in place. We also decide how the agreement will be drawn up and encapsulated.

Starting the discussions

You are probably wondering how you can do this yourself, without an independent person assisting you. I have provided you with my framework in this book, and I honestly believe that if there is a true desire to be amicable, you can do this on your own.

> **Tip**
>
> If things get a little tough and you just can't do it then there is nothing wrong with going to a mediator or kind lawyer to assist you.

If you do go it alone, just follow my process. Firstly, prepare your opening statements and then work together to set a suitable agenda.

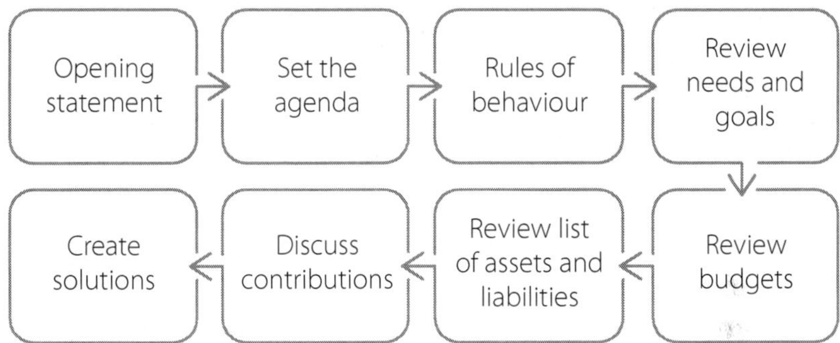

Open the discussion

In a mediation setting, I ask the parties to tell each other what they are here for and what they want to achieve. Let's call it an opening statement. It's a really great way to set the scene and make sure that you each know why you are there.

Here are the most common reasons that are given:

1. They want to calmly discuss and resolve their settlement.
2. They want to avoid court and spending lots of money on lawyers and court fees.

3. They want to walk away with their relationship intact so that they can communicate well in the future for the sake of the children.
4. They want to make sure the other one is well looked after.

You can easily do this. Explain why you are here and what you are hoping to achieve. Do note that this is not the time for stories, outcomes or accusations. This is a simple statement of what you are hoping to get out of your discussions.

Set an agenda

Task 13

Create a joint agenda.

You now need to create an agenda and list all the things that you need to talk about and get resolved. The reason for this is to make sure you both remember the things that you need to talk about through the entire process.

Go back and look at the list you created at stage 2; is there anything on there you still need to talk about? You should have created a list of the most important issues you needed to talk about and resolve. These can be interim or long term.

Start this conversation by taking turns, and add whatever you have listed. Read off the list of items that you have created and then the other party should do the same.

More often than not they are very similar.

I often use a big piece of butcher's paper but you can use my agenda items list below.

Agenda items

Priority	Item	Completed

Once you have this, let's look at prioritising these items so that you know where to start. Once they are completed, mark them off.

The purpose of an agenda is to make sure that you both talk about all the things you need to and also to make sure that you don't forget or miss anything. It also helps keep you on track.

If you are having trouble thinking of things, here are a few standard inclusions that show up in my meditations.

Agenda items

Priority	Item	Completed
1	The agreed rules of behaviour	
2	Review each other's needs and goals	
3	Review your individual budgets	
4	Explore each other's goals, issues and needs	
5	Create an agreed list of Assets and Liabilities	
6	Create solutions	

Task 14

Start working through your agenda.

If you are doing it alone, use your agenda and my tips to guide you through. Just take it one item at a time.

Rules of behaviour

This should be relatively easy. Consider whatever feels comfortable for you. What are the behaviours you want each other to avoid?

This purpose of this task as the number one priority is to ensure that you are both responsible for your own behaviour and keep each other on task.

As hard as this is going to be, it is so much harder and things break down so very quickly if one of you is behaving badly. This is where you make a commitment to each other to follow the process, stay calm and behave. You have come so far; it is so important that bad behaviour doesn't derail you.

Review needs and goals

Earlier I asked you both to list your values and reasons for being there and what you are hoping to achieve. You also created a list of the things that are really important to you. These are your needs and your goals. The things that you think you need to move on and move forward. You now need to go through these together.

I am not asking you to list outcomes here; don't say, 'I want to get 60% of the pool of assets.' This is about the reasons you are choosing to do this together. This will be those items like:

1. I need a roof over my head for the children.
2. I want the children to stay in private school.
3. I need the larger vehicle as I have to transport the kids to and from school.

It is really important here to go where it feels *uncomfortable*; be truly open and honest so that your ex-partner can really listen and know what you need.

Review budgets

If you have both been following the process, you should each have a clear budget.

The point of a budget is so that the other person is very clear on what you can and cannot afford. They need to know what financial position you are in.

It may be that you need to show proof of your income with your most recent payslips. This is the best way to explain and prove what your income is so that your ex-partner has a very good understanding of what you have available. If you are receiving benefits then show them your most recent statement of benefits.

You will also need to carefully look at expenses together. You may have doubled up on some items, such as health insurance, mortgage payments or school fees. It may be that you can agree on who will pay some of those items moving forward.

The other main benefit of having clear and accurate budgets is so that you each know what financial resources you have to make decisions about, who should pay for what, and who can ultimately afford to keep assets or take over mortgages when you get to solutions.

Obviously, you may need to come back and change your budget when you reach an agreement. If you are keeping the house and taking over the mortgage, then you will need to make sure your budget reflects this.

Discuss contributions

During step 4 you created a list of all the things you would like considered. These were your initial contributions, all the things that you both did during the relationship and also what your needs are for the future.

I often find this a difficult discussion, but totally necessary. The key here is to remember that you don't have to agree on all of these contributions, you just need to consider them. If there is anything you are unsure about, say your ex-partner says he put in $150,000 from an inheritance and you through it was only $60,000, see what homework you both need to do to clarify. Perhaps a copy of the estate distribution or bank deposit will help. Often these things can be cleared up easily.

This is also not a time to fight or disagree. It is a discussion. Keep it simple. Get more information if you need to.

The idea of this stage is to make sure everything is clarified, and then you can decide later when looking at options whether you need to adjust any outcome as a result of these considerations.

Review list of assets and liabilities and values

You should both have your own list of assets and liabilities. The first thing you need to do is compare the items you have included.

I would start with a fresh blank schedule and insert the assets you have both listed. The purpose of using a blank list is so that you can add anything else that you may each have missed on your own list. I start with simply listing the items first, then we can go to values.

Use the following schedule.

Asset	Description	Value	Liability	Equity
Bank account				
Savings account				
Matrimonial home				
Furniture				
Shares				
Motor vehicle 1				
Motor vehicle 2				
			Total asset pool	$

<table>
<tr><th rowspan="2">Superannuation</th><th rowspan="2">Fund name</th><th colspan="2">Value</th></tr>
<tr><th>At cohabitation</th><th>Present</th></tr>
<tr><td>Party A's account</td><td></td><td></td><td></td></tr>
<tr><td>Party B's account</td><td></td><td></td><td></td></tr>
<tr><td></td><td></td><td></td><td></td></tr>
<tr><td></td><td></td><td></td><td></td></tr>
<tr><td></td><td>Total superannuation</td><td>$</b></td><td><b>$</td></tr>
</table>

Once you have both written all of the items down, you can then start to consider the values. This is also the time when you may need to use any of the documents that you have collected.

Let's look at a few items closely.

House

List the address of the house, and if you have a rates notice handy also list the title description.

Next you will need to talk about the value. If you completed stage 3 then you are each likely to have a good idea of the value. You have either obtained an appraisal from a real estate agent or a formal valuation.

Compare the value that you each have. If it is the same, then wonderful – you can agree on that value and insert. If, however, you have differing values, then you will need to discuss the best way to reach an agreement as to the value.

Often clients who have real estate appraisals rather than formal valuations will find that they have a larger variety in their values. I would suggest here that, if you do not already have a formal valuation, and you can't agree on a value, then you both agree to appoint a valuer.

Tip

You should both look into who you would like to do the valuation. Take into consideration their experience, price and report turnaround time. You should both agree on who does this so there is no argument as to any bias.

You should also decide who will contact the valuer and ask for a joint valuation.

Once you have either agreed on a value or received the joint valuation, then you can insert the value into your table. This may take place at a later meeting.

Now at the same time, consider any debt that may be against the property. Normally this is simply your mortgage, which you can check via your online banking or most recent statement that you should have at hand. Insert that value.

Now let's work out the equity in your house. That is, the agreed value of the house less the mortgage and any other debts attached to the house. Most commonly this looks like this:

House: 1 Smith Street, Melbourne	$500,000
Mortgage: NAB Loan 123456	$200,000
Equity	$300,000

Bank accounts

Your bank account balances are easy. The key is again to remember that you have to list everything. Insert every account that each of you has either in your own name, joint names or with anyone else. List the bank, account number and balance:

NAB Account: 987654 balance	$2.00
WPC Account: 564562 balance	$2,523.00

This is the time when you show each other your statements and current balances to establish what funds you have in those accounts.

Motor vehicles

List the make and model of any vehicles. You need to list all vehicles that either of you have.

For example, let's say you have a Toyota Corolla and your ex-partner a Nissan Navara. List them both, then pull out that registration papers you have and insert the registration details.

You may have chosen to take a guess at the value, and this is the time to talk about these values and see if you can agree. Hopefully, you have a little more information and have used the Redbook valuation system talked about in stage 3, but if not, this is the time that you and your ex-partner agree to do this together. Login to www.redbook.com.au and insert all the vehicles details. Hopefully, you can then jointly use this information to agree upon and insert a value.

Again, we also need to work out the equity. You should have your loan details or lease payout figure, and you can show this to your ex, agree upon and insert a value.

It should look a little like this:

	Value	Debt	Equity
Toyota Corolla 2010 GHY123	$20,000	$2,500	$17,500
Nissan Navara 2012 HYG654	$25,000	$0	$25,000

Other items

I have just gone through some common assets, but remember, go through your own list that was created in stage 3 and make sure you have discussed and inserted all of the items that you had listed.

Sometimes couples agree not to insert an item; perhaps you listed an old trailer and it is now only worth $500 and you both agree that this can be left out or is of nil value. That's okay; the point here is to make sure you have listed everything that is relevant, and it has either an agreed value or you have agreed how to value it.

Finalising the value of the pool of assets

This is the easy part. Once you have finished agreeing upon all of the assets and liabilities and their respective values, you simply need to add them all up and work out the total value. This is what we call the value of your 'pool of assets'.

What happens when your finances are complicated?

I've had clients where this stage was far too complicated for them. The reasons behind this are usually that their finances are overly complicated and/or are usually handled by the accountant and/or financial planner and/or there are some tricky legal issues.

If this is the case, then I simply suggest you go back to them and engage them jointly to assist you. Ask them to produce a detailed list of your assets and liabilities. Explain that you need each item listed individually and they need to include values.

If it is really tricky, invite the accountant and/or financial planner to your joint meeting and you can all work together to settle the value of the pool of assets and even get them to help you create a tax-effective and smart plan for your new futures.

Creating solutions

All your hard work, preparation and thought is now going to be put to good use. Remember, you have already prepared for this part at step 4 where you created a list of possible outcomes.

The best practice is to simply work through it together. It may be easy to delete some of the suggestions after reviewing budgets and your earlier discussion.

Go through step by step each option you have come up with and work through the pros and cons. You also need to go back to the task of reality testing each option. Often that will help you come up with the solutions or even create new ones.

You do need to consider your contributions and your needs and also those of your ex-spouse. Place yourself in their shoes and make sure you consider this from all angles.

If you have come this far then it is because you want to do this amicably and in a kind and calm way. You most definitely need to be very open now and make sure that you frankly talk about all options. Stick to your values so that at all times you are following the most positive path for you.

Two of our couples managed to stay on track and were easily able to get to the negotiation stage all on their own.

Couple 4: Monica and Tim

They discussed their situation and agree that they both accumulated their wealth together and that no one person contributed more.

Monica admits to Tim that she really doesn't want to keep the house, that she just doesn't think she can afford it. Tim explains that it would be preferable for him to keep it as he really doesn't want to have to move and he has his shed all set up and doesn't want to have to do that again. He has spoken to the bank and he can borrow an amount of $300,000. This would mean that he can pay out the joint mortgage of $200,000 and he can also pay Monica a lump sum of $100,000 for her share in the property.

He suggests that as their assets are valued at $220,000 that it would be fair that they each get half, being $110,000 each. Monica suggests that she would keep her car which is only valued at $10,000, and the $100,000 payment and that would achieve the $110,000 for her.

Tim is very pleased with this, and he is happy to agree to finalise things on that basis. They both agree that they think it best to have this agreement written up by someone professional and they could split the cost of this.

Couple 2: Jennifer and William

Once they had everything together Jennifer went to her bank to see what she could borrow. She thought it was unlikely she would get loan approval on her income, and her banker thought it unlikely William would either due to his injury and compensation. It seemed to her that it was likely the house would have to sell.

Jennifer organised to meet with William. She arranged for her parents to look after the girls so that they could have uninterrupted time. Jennifer explained all that she had learnt from the lawyer and told William that she wanted to try to sort this out themselves. William said he was agreeable to this.

Jennifer showed him all of the documents she had gathered and also her draft schedule of assets and liabilities. They went through each item together and were able to agree on the majority of the items listed. Jennifer also explained to him that she had spoken to the bank and didn't think that either of them could keep the house. William agreed that there was no way he could get a loan until his back issue was resolved. He agreed that although it saddened him, the house would have to be sold and they would each have to rent until they could afford otherwise.

William suggested that he could see no reason as to why the house shouldn't be split 50% to each of them, especially considering they were going to be sharing the care and cost of the girls. They agreed that the house would be sold and the proceeds of sale divided evenly after they paid out the mortgage.

Tip

Make sure you follow my advice and separate the meetings and don't try to do it all in one go.

Doing it with a little help

What happens if you get stuck?

Getting to a sticky point is common. This is where we need to stay really calm and think practically. What is the issue? What is it you are getting stuck on? If you need to take a break and come back another day, do that. Or perhaps things are even harder than that and you need to get some more external advice? In my collaborative mediation process, I often send couples off to get some independent legal advice if they are stuck on an issue.

So, if you have hit a legal issue or you are just going around in circles, perhaps it's time to call on that kind lawyer for some advice. Tell them where you are and what the problem is and get some solid advice on your options. If it's a legal issue such as paying back a loan to parents, or how to treat an inheritance, I would strongly suggest you both get some independent advice. Often, if you are both seeing experienced family lawyers you will get the correct advice that will help you reach a solution. You can then come back together and explain what advice you obtained, and most times the parties realise the best outcome and can move past that stage.

If you really can't sit down together

My goal is to educate and teach couples that they can do this together. If they follow the Peaceful Pathway then they can create their own solutions.

However, there are times when they just can't.

If this is the case then I suggest you consider that calm and kind lawyer who can guide you. Ask them to advise you on mediation options and collaborative practice (I explain both of these in more detail in the previous chapter). We are fighting for a calm and peaceful solution and there is more than one path there. As long as it is a peaceful path then you are winning that fight.

Step 6
Finalise

'Peace of mind is attained not by ignoring problems, but by solving them.'

Raymond Hull

The final check and wrap up

My hope right now is that you have come up with a fantastic solution that you both feel happy and comfortable with. This final stage of my process is all about wrapping things up, making your agreement final, and putting those final touches in.

The relief when you have reached that agreement is incredible. There is always so much pressure and stress to work out an agreement, and when that pressure is released you will start to see a noticeably clear and peaceful path ahead. This final step is to ensure that the agreement you have will not only work but will remain a valid and realistic agreement so that there is no confusion going forward, and also to make sure it is written up correctly.

The first step here is to make sure that you have all bases covered. Have you considered what will happen if your plan A does not work? Do you have a plan B?

I had a lovely new client call me the other day; he was a referral from a couple I had assisted in the past. He said to me that he and his wife had separated, they had an amicable agreement and were really just wanting my assistance to formalise the agreement that they had reached at mediation. Great. Well, when I delved into the agreement, I realised that there were a few problems. Even thought they had agreed the wife would take over the house, it appeared unlikely she would get finance to do so, and they had no plan if that didn't happen. When we talked about this, their amicable demeanour started to become the opposite. Their frustrations took over. They fell back into terrible language, bad behaviour, and really weren't thinking about each other at all.

The point here is that in the absence of a clear plan A and a fallback plan B, conflict arose, and they struggled to stay on track after starting out peacefully.

The best thing you can do now is make sure that although you feel you have a great agreement in place, we need to test it a little, and have an alternative position, just in case. This Peaceful Pathway is all about avoiding conflicts and creating clear and precise positive avenues to follow. You really do not want to get to this stage of the process and end up arguing to the point where you then both veer off this path, get litigious and start down that dark avenue. I am determined to keep you on track till then end.

Another thing to remember here is that you should still, as you should in every stage, go back and review your behaviour standards and your values, and stay on the positive path. If you need some advice at this stage, by all means, I encourage it. Just remember any professional that you do seek help from should also pass your rules and follow your values. You are still the leader on this pathway and you make the choices.

The second step on this stage is to make sure you are both on the same page when it comes to how to finalise your agreement. Have you both considered how you want to draw it up? Do you even want to draw it up? Make sure you have considered and agreed on all aspects.

What you need to consider if you reach an agreement

So, what's next? You have reached an agreement, that is fantastic. I know what hard work it is to get to this point. It is a huge accomplishment, so be very, very proud of where you are right now. You are so very close now.

In order to finish things off and wrap it all up, this final stage requires you to both take a really good look at the agreement you have reached and work out what you both have to do in order to make that agreement a reality. We need to check it will work, that you have a fallback position and have timeframes set.

Consideration 1: compliance

Can you actually comply with the terms of the agreement?

You've reached an agreement with your ex-spouse that you will take over the current home loan and pay your ex out. What is the exact amount you need? Hopefully, you have taken my advice and done your homework at stage 3 and have an indicative approval from the bank, and you've used this amount to work out your agreement.

Now is the time to go back to the bank with the final amount and make sure that this amount is still available. You need to get confirmation that you can borrow the exact amount you need and comply with the agreement.

Perhaps it is not a loan approval? It could be something else. Have a good think about all aspects of your agreement and make sure that you can actually do it.

Some likely items may be:

- obtain finance approval for the amount required
- make sure you know the repayment amounts and that you can afford this
- obtain finance approval for any other refinancing obligations such as vehicles
- check the final payout for a debt – make sure it is still accurate.

Consideration 2: fallback positions

Do you remember the story I told you at the start of this chapter, the one where the couple's agreement started to crumble when they realised it just wouldn't work? That was a perfect example of why you should always also have a fallback position. Right now is the time to discuss and agree on a fall-back position.

To put it simply, when I talk about a fall-back position this means a plan B if the first plan or solution doesn't work. What happens if your circumstances have changed and you can't get that loan anymore, or the bank requirements have changed and you no longer qualify? Do you have an alternative solution? The worst thing that can happen is that there is no fallback position and all of your hard work falls over and there is no plan agreed to move forward.

Another simple example of this is that I had an elderly couple a few years back that had entered into an agreement a year before. The agreement from their point of view was quite simple: the parties were to list the house for sale, and they would share the proceeds. Simple.

The husband agreed he would stay in the house and look after it until it was sold. The problem they had is that the bottom fell out of the market and the house wouldn't sell. The wife thought that perhaps they should just auction it and just take what they could get and move on. The husband, who was living comfortably in the house, did not agree; he wanted to get maximum value and was happy to wait it out.

The problem they faced is that they didn't consider the possibility the house would take so long to sell. The solution to this problem would have been to have thought through the worst-case scenarios before they signed off on any agreement. They could have agreed then and there that they would need to auction it, or come up with another plan.

Another option could have been an option to buy out. Perhaps one of them may have been in a better financial position 12 months later and could have bought the other one out.

There are many other solutions; you just need to make sure that you always have a back-up plan in case the first plan doesn't eventuate, and always put a timeframe on it.

Consideration 3: timeframes

Another weak point of that couple's agreement was that they had no timeframe. If they had agreed right at the start that they would wait 12 months for a private sale, and if it didn't happen they would place it up for auction, then they would not have faced this problem. Nothing worse than having to sit and wait for an unknown period as you didn't set a schedule.

So, sit down, brainstorm, and make sure that part of your agreement includes a fallback position if your plan A doesn't work out, and it has a timeframe linked to every step.

Task 15

Review your agreement and evaluate all of the above considerations.

The agreement

What to do once you have all the terms of your agreement

Having carefully thought through your agreement and having made sure you have a fallback position and timeframe agreed, you can now move forward and have your agreement formalised.

You have several options here:

- write up an informal agreement
- enter into consent orders
- have a binding financial agreement written up by a lawyer.

Now if you are feeling a little insecure about what to do here, then again, seek some advice and support from a professional who has the correct knowledge and experience. There are a few ways you can move forward here, and it will depend on what you are both wanting.

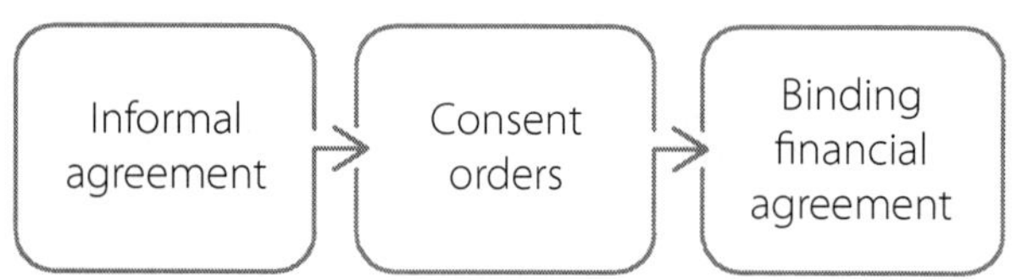

Briefly I will explain the differences.

Informal agreement

I have seen these done in all manner or ways; some couples simply write it up in their own language and sign off on it. I have seen emails back and forward confirming what they have agreed and how they will move forward. Remember, this is in no way legally binding and cannot be relied upon to enforce your agreement; it is more of the old handshake agreement and is completely informal. In some cases, that is all the parties want.

Consent orders

A consent order is simply that. An order that is made by the court with your consent. You prepare an application document for the Magistrate to consider your position; this includes all your financial information, and sets out the agreement you have reached. The Magistrate uses this information to review your agreement and ultimately decides if it appears fair and reasonable. The Magistrate then signs off on the order you have prepared, and this will be your guide moving forward. Once the order is made, it is legally binding, and both parties have a legal obligation to comply.

You can attempt to do this yourself, or there is assistance out there which I will explain below, or you can seek the assistance of a lawyer to prepare your application.

Binding financial agreement

This is a formal document that is prepared by lawyers under the terms of the Family Law Act. It does not have to be approved by the court, but it does require both parties to obtain independent legal advice.

Once completed, and completed correctly, it too will be legally binding.

A closer look at your options

Option 1: write up yourself

If you want to do this all by yourself, then your options here are to elect for an informal agreement or have a go at doing your own application for consent orders. You cannot do a binding financial agreement unless you both seek legal advice, so you cannot do this yourself.

Informal agreement

Doing it yourself? Although we lawyers are always wary of this, if you are on an amicable path and do not intend to seek any further professional advice, you can simply write it down, agree to it and stop there. The risk is that as it is not legally binding the agreement cannot be enforced. On the other hand, I know plenty of couples that had no real reason to write it up as they did not need to transfer any assets or had no fear of future claims. They just split it all up and moved on, never to look back. There are always ongoing risks here, such as future claims against your assets, but if you are informed and fully aware of potential problems, this is still a choice you can make.

Consent orders

Are you feeling you need a little more security? If you are feeling that you want your agreement to be a little more formal, but are still wanting to avoid getting advice to write it up professionally, you can actually try preparing your legal documents yourself.

When I started law, if someone had said that to me, I would have been in utter shock. 'What?!' I would have said. 'Are you *crazy*? Why would you write up your own legal documents – whoever does that is in for a world of trouble.' Now remember, I have seen a lot more now and I also know that this is how I was taught to respond and trained to protect clients at all costs. Life has taught me that the 'lawyer' is not always the only way.

In fact, with all of the artificial intelligence out there, there are indeed several programs and even online firms available that will assist you to write up your own consent orders without even having to see anyone or pay large sums of money. It is very low cost.

What you are doing here is getting a guide or a precedent that will satisfy the requirements of the court, then you can submit your agreement to be approved by the Magistrate.

You can have a look at www.familycourt.gov.au – Do it Yourself Kits, specifically the application for consent orders. The only cost here is the filing fee, which is $170 at the time of writing.

You could go a little further and try www.edivorce.com.au – they allow you to complete an online form and they upload your information to prepare your documents. This is a little more expensive, as they charge a fee of $249, and once again you will still pay the filing fee.

There are also some law firms that are moving to the low cost, artificial intelligence model to help create your documents quickly and at lower cost to the traditional, face-to-face appointments. This might be worth looking into also.

Always remember however that if you have a tricky agreement or you have concerns, there is no problem with checking your concerns with a suitable lawyer and seeking some guidance. You have done all the hard work so far. You do not necessarily have to engage them in the process; you can just seek advice on the best way forward.

Timeframes

Just a little reminder here on timeframes: if you are in a de facto relationship then you have two years from the date of your separation to finalise any formal agreement. If you were married this is 12 months from the date you were divorced. So, whatever way you choose, just make sure you have decided before your time expires.

Option 2: lawyer to assist in writing it up

Where to go

Amicable couples commonly work together to have their agreement formalised by a lawyer. Just because you choose to get a lawyer doesn't mean that you are not still being amicable. Assisting clients to finalise an agreement that they reached on their own, or with a mediator, is a huge part of my business.

Some couples just want that little comfort blanket to know that this is final, and they can move on. Almost like closing one door before you can open another.

Frankly, when they do come to me at this point it is much more pleasant. At this point they have already done all the hard work, they have an agreement, and they just want it formalised by someone other than themselves and don't want the added stress. Some clients simply hate paperwork and just want someone else to sort that last step for them. Certainly, as all the hard work is done, it costs a lot less and can be completed quickly.

Make sure that whatever lawyer you do choose is one who fits your bill. The last thing you want is to engage a litigious lawyer who talks you out of your well-thought-out, well-researched, and carefully considered agreement. I am not bashing lawyers here – I am a lawyer – but in the last 15 years I have come across some difficult situations where possibly more in-depth or calm advice could have been offered and would have resulted in a much better outcome.

On a more positive note, and more frequently, I have met and worked very closely with some of the most amazing, kind-hearted people who are family lawyers and do just want to help. This is who you are after here – great advice with a personal understanding.

Jennifer and William chose wisely.

Couple 2: Jennifer and William

Jennifer offered that she would go back to this lawyer and ask him to write up the documents. William was happy with this and said he would be happy to pay half of the costs. He said he didn't intend to get a lawyer as he didn't feel the need. So Jennifer arranged for the settlement documents to be prepared by her kind lawyer.

He then phoned and emailed William a few times to obtain the balance of the information that he needed to prepare the documents, and William commented to Jennifer how helpful and kind the lawyer was to him. He had always thought that her lawyer couldn't speak to him, however the lawyer explained that there was no issue with speaking to him, unless he had his own lawyer of course, then he couldn't. The only issue was he couldn't give him legal advice. William was very happy with this and still felt comfortable in not needing his own legal advice.

The key for William and Jennifer is that Jennifer was able to find a great lawyer who gave her some really good guidance and advice. She was not immediately led into any angry letter writing, litigation or arguments. She was given information as to how to prepare herself and she was then able to carefully negotiate on her own. She did go back to the lawyer to have the agreement written up, and could have gone back to ask questions if she needed, so she felt very supported throughout the entire process. Her lawyer was also kind and considerate to William, which was needed in the circumstances. This option was very low stress and low cost (which was shared) and it only took a few weeks. Of course it was very much led by some very calm and peaceful behaviour by both William and Jennifer.

Consent orders

If you are looking at choosing to prepare consent orders through a lawyer then only one of you really 'needs' to go to a lawyer to get this written up. There is no 'requirement' as such for you both having to get legal advice. The aim here is to get someone with the skill and knowledge to write up a legally binding document. Unless of course you have any concerns, the other can most certainly seek advice and support too.

Once the application is prepared on your behalf, you both read over it, arrange to sign it, and then the lawyer will file with the court physically or online. You don't actually need to attend. The Magistrate does all of this in chambers, so no fear that you have to get dressed up and sit before the Magistrate.

Binding financial agreement

If you decide you want to enter into a binding financial agreement then you will both need a lawyer. It is most common for one party to instruct the lawyer to prepare the document and the other simply to get the independent advice on the agreement that is drafted. Again, choose your lawyers carefully. Your lawyer will give you all the advice you need to make sure you understand the advantages and disadvantages of entering into a binding financial agreement.

Couple 4: Monica and Tim

Monica, being the organiser, has agreed to call a solicitor. She knows that she is after a solicitor who is experienced in family law but also uses kinder and more amicable methods to work through family law. She therefore avoids litigation-style lawyers. She knows that she really just needs to find someone who can prepare the settlement documents and explain anything she may need to know about them.

Monica calls a firm that has been recommended to her by a good friend, and she has a quick telephone meeting with the lawyer. The lawyer confirms that she can indeed assist her with preparation of her documents, and she suggests that they do this by way of a binding financial agreement. She explains that she can prepare the documents on behalf of Monica, and Tim will need to obtain his own independent advice. She does, however, suggest a good lawyer that she works well with and recommends that he see them for the independent advice.

Ultimately, the documents are prepared and explained to Monica, and she is very happy to go ahead. Tim does engage the lawyer suggested by Monica's lawyer, and they also explain and advise him on the documents. He feels comfortable the agreement is fair. He signs off on the documents.

Moncia's solicitor assists them in the transfer and the refinance, and the process is very calm and smooth. Both Monica and Tim are very happy with the process and the outcome, which was quick, cost effective and very peaceful.

The key here is knowing how you want to draw up your agreement and then choosing the correct pathway for you and your family.

Your final task:

Task 16

Decide how you want to encapsulate your agreement and get it done.

Other pathways

'Sometimes the right path is not always the easiest one.'

Anonymous

What happens if we can't reach an agreement?

Despite all your best intentions, sometimes couples just can't get to an agreement without a little extra help and support. Do not be disillusioned; there are still options to stay on the Peaceful Path. There can be many reasons for this; perhaps there are just still too many emotions to deal with, or your circumstances are tricky or complicated. There is nothing wrong with this – it's common.

Think of it this way: you have done all of the hard work, you are well and truly prepared, ready to continue negotiating, you just need a little more help at this stage, some extra special support. There is still a peaceful pathway ahead for you. The important thing here is to choose the best path for *you*. The best possible paths you can choose here are either mediation or collaborative practice.

There is no failure here. Engaging a mediator to assist you in your negotiations is a great option and would be my number one go-to choice. The success rate of agreements following mediation is extremely high.

If mediation isn't right for you, or you have a complicated matter for which having lawyers present would be more comforting, then moving to a collaborative practice setting, in my experience, would be the next step that should follow.

Both options should be investigated fully. We are still doing all we can here to avoid that litigious setting.

Mediation

Mediation is a fabulous option. I love mediation and I love being a mediator. Mediation is still all about being amicable, creating your own solutions and being interest focused.

If you have either attempted to negotiate on your own or you are struggling to do it alone, then make some enquiries and get a few referrals for a great mediator, someone again who suits you and your style.

The mediation process is similar to what you have already been guided through; including a mediator at this stage is taking you a little further by including an experienced, independent person to assist you with the negotiations.

I will say it again: I truly love mediation. I have developed my own unique mediation process, which is slightly different to the way some mediators do it, by simply breaking down the steps (just as I have in this book). It's all about preparing, gathering all the information, and reviewing and exploring your options.

No matter what stage you were able to get to on your own, it is well worth the hard work, the anguish and money you have saved through these steps. You will have completed many of the hard steps; you may just need that independent person to help you along to reach the end. Perfectly fine.

How do I choose a mediator?

When looking for a mediator, you should be looking for someone with family law experience. There are many great mediators out there, but it is definitely a benefit to choose one who is well versed in family law mediations. They have the experience and knowledge to work through your assets and liabilities and also to help you look through your contributions and future needs.

What is the process?

Once you have chosen your mediator you will participate in an intake session. This may differ from mediator to mediator, but it essentially involves the mediator checking to make sure your matter is actually suitable for mediation and getting some basic information from you and explaining the rules and process.

You will also be asked to sign a mediation agreement, which also includes a confidentiality agreement. The reason for this is so that you can both feel free to speak openly without fear that your words or discussions may be used against you.

Once your matter has been deemed suitable your mediator will move you into your joint sessions. Now each individual mediator will do this a bit differently, but as I mentioned earlier, I split this into several sessions and break down the stages that we need to go through. Depending on the level of service you are paying for, it may just be one joint session where you work through your issues in an attempt to reach an agreement.

If you have worked through the first part of this guide yourself, then you will be well prepared, have all of the required information and the process can commence smoothly.

Once you have finished with your mediator, hopefully you have an agreement in hand and you can keep moving through this process to prepare an agreement as set out in the final stage of my process.

Frank and Joan utilised a mediator.

Couple 5: Frank and Joan

Frank has made arrangements for he and Joan to see a private mediator. She was recommended to him by the lawyer he saw. The mediator then contacts both parties to conduct their intake session. This intake simply consists of a basic discussion with the mediator where both Joan and Frank separately have a conversation about their circumstances, their needs and their goals. The mediator also explains the process to make sure they understand the rules and the process, and that she can get to know them better.

After their intake sessions both Frank and Joan sit down with the mediator in a joint session.

Joan is very worried about what the future holds for her, but one thing she is sure of is that she cannot keep and maintain their big house. It is far too big for her, and she really doesn't want to have to maintain something that large. She is also very keen to move to Queensland as both of their daughters are now living there and she wants to be close to them. She doesn't care if Frank wants to keep the house.

Frank is not too concerned about his financial future. His business is functioning well, and he has a good income. He has also decided that although he can probably afford to keep the house, it is probably not what he needs. He thinks something smaller would be more suitable for him; he doesn't spend too much time at home anyway.

Frank has always been the one who organises the finances, so he is well prepared and already had a folder handy with all the documents they needed. He had also prepared a budget. The mediator had indicated to him that the more information he has the better. He also made a detailed list of all of their assets and liabilities to go with the folder that had all of the relating information.

On the day of mediation Frank and Joan turn up separately. They are led into a mediation room where they are joined by the mediator. The mediator sets an agenda for them and they then start working through their options. Frank is very well prepared, so they are very quickly and easily able to agree on and sort out values for their assets. They only value Frank was not sure about was the value for the house.

Both parties quickly realise that the value of the house is not an issue as neither one wants to keep it. They agree that it should be listed for sale as soon as possible and are both happy to use their usual real estate agent.

The mediator takes them through a discussion where they both agree that there have been no major or significant contributions compared to the other. They met very young, and although Joan took time off when the girls were young, she took care of the children and the home while Frank worked. Neither of them had any lump sums of cash or other large assets, and they both just worked hard to be where they are now.

Frank is a little concerned about Joan's future and wants to make sure she is looked after. He has a particularly good income but Joan will need to find another job to support herself. Joan suggests that they just sell and split the proceeds of the sale of the house and divide everything 50%. Frank knows that there is about $100,000 in their term deposit and suggests that as he has a good income and he will have significant funds from his half of the sale of the house that Joan also keeps the term deposit. That way she should have enough to buy herself a unit in Queensland and also have some money there until she can get a job. Joan is very happy with this.

They end up agreeing that this is the best way forward. The mediator writes up their agreement in dot point form and they both sign it. Frank agrees that he will take it to the lawyer he saw and ask her to write it up. Joan says that she will either go back to the lawyer that she first saw or find someone else.

Within two weeks they have a carefully drafted application and terms of settlement and they both sign and file it in court.

Frank and Joan, having been very close to veering off the Peaceful Pathway at the start, were very happy with the outcome. The only expense to them was the joint cost of the mediator and the preparation of the documents. Their relationship, although still a little strained, is in good shape, and they both feel they can peacefully move on. Their story shows that it is so very important to get good advice, explore all of your options, and make sure you are in control of the process.

If mediation is not suitable or doesn't work, my next go-to option is collaborative practice. This involves a lawyer, but in my opinion is the most peaceful path you can take when using lawyers.

Lawyer-led negotiation – collaborative practice

Most people have never heard of 'collaborative legal practice'. I recently heard collaborative practice referred to as a 'new method' of family lawyering. Well, it isn't. Collaborative practice has in fact been around for some time; it is just that it's not as commonly used.

The reason it is not so common, sadly, is because it requires lawyers to sign an agreement that they will not proceed to represent you in court if you do not settle. This means if you don't settle, they cannot represent you and you need to get another lawyer, and the lawyer loses the client and the work. We must not forget however, that the lawyers in the first instance are doing all they can to assist you in a kind and calm way and the majority of these negotiations settle and never need to consider court anyway. There are many other reasons why lawyers won't agree to this, some simply because they are litigation lawyers and well trained in that area and are sticking to that skill, others are unaware or uneducated as to the process.

If you do choose this option and find a collaboratively trained lawyer, the benefit of this is that the parties feel more comfortable that the lawyers are working with them to reach a solution and are not thinking about encouraging litigation. It also allows the parties to speak freely and openly in front of the other lawyer about their situation, without the fear that their words will be used against them in court.

No one can argue with me here that a lawyer makes a great deal more if the matter were to be litigated and they spend hundreds of hours preparing for and attending court. If they do get instructed to do this work then they have every right to charge for it. However, if agreements can be reached early, there are no litigation costs. Our aim here is to stay on the Peaceful Pathway, avoiding the negative and costly path, so why not try collaborative practice? It really works. Spread the word.

How does collaborative practice work exactly?

So, what exactly is it? Collaborative practice involves each party obtaining a lawyer (one trained in the collaborative method) then sitting down as a team of four to work things out. Each party and their lawyers are involved in discussing the assets, liabilities and contributions, then coming up with solutions. It really is a great process.

The beauty of this method is that it also encompasses a lot of the tools that I have given you. You go through similar steps during the collaborative process. We also often invite other professionals to join into my mediation meetings (if that would be useful), such as accountants, financial planners or counsellors, all working together to reach an agreement.

We all work together as a team, there are rules of behaviour, and we really do speak openly and freely to each other. The lawyers can talk to the other party's client, there are no accusations or claims being thrown around – it's about being kind and calm and trying to work out the best way to assist the couple.

This really is a peaceful way to work things out if you are having difficulties doing it alone or your finances or circumstances are just too complicated to do it without legal advice.

If you have come this far and you have no agreement, your attempts to negotiate have failed, your mediation has failed – this is another fantastic peaceful path to follow.

Tip

Choose your lawyer wisely.

You will need to make sure that the lawyer you use has been trained in the collaborative method and they are indeed aiming for a calm and peaceful solution for you. Get them to explain how they use the process, their experience, and what it costs. You should get a good idea of their personality and professional process before you engage them.

Finally, our couple Jane and Peter were able to utilise this process wisely.

Couple 3: Jane and Peter

Jane made the appointment with the lawyer and immediately knew she had made the right choice. Her lawyer explained the collaborative process very clearly and alleviated Jane's concerns. The lawyer noted that at all times they would be working as a team, that she would be kind, calm and respectful towards Peter and the lawyer he would choose. She suggested that Jane email Peter with the suggestion to use the collaborative method, and she gave her a few names of other lawyers who were like minded, were trained in collaborative work and would work well with them.

After receiving the email Peter decided he would also like to follow this path. He contacted one of the lawyers that had been suggested. After speaking with the lawyer, he too liked the idea of working collaboratively and engaged the solicitor to start the process.

Now that Peter and Jane were in the collaborative setting, they went through step 3 – gathering information – with their lawyers. This was done in a joint meeting where the four of them sat down and worked out all the information they would need to create their budgets and schedule of assets and liabilities. They also made things easier by using electronic documents, and shared those with each other so that they didn't have huge bundles of paper. The lawyers then helped them prepare their schedule.

They were also able to collectively agree on how to value the house. They decided to jointly engage a valuer, and agreed that whatever the value was that came back would be the value that they would negotiate on.

The rest of the assets were relatively easy to work out, and they were able to simply agree on what value they should attribute to those items.

Within two meetings they were able to have an agreed schedule of assets and liabilities, and had ticked off and viewed all of the relevant documents relating to those assets.

Jane and Peter were also advised by their lawyers to talk to their bank or their broker to look into their own lending capacity, so that when they started discussions on outcomes they would know what they may be able to afford.

After having created their schedule, the parties met again for a joint meeting to start discussing needs and options.

Jane indicated that she really wanted to stay in the house. She felt that this would provide security and stability for her and the kids, and would create less disruption. Peter agreed that he thought this was important, and he also wanted to try to reach an outcome that would allow Jane and the kids to stay in the house.

Peter did indicate that he would have to initially rent something, but as he would like space for the kids, he would long term like to make sure he had a deposit for a house.

With the help of the lawyers, both Jane and Peter were able to come up with some good solutions and ultimately were able to agree on Jane keeping the house and that she would pay Peter out a lump sum and take over the mortgage. This meant she would have to take out a larger mortgage in her own name, but she had approval from her bank to do so.

With the help of the lawyers, there was one final joint meeting to go through the final terms of the agreement. Jane and Peter, with the lawyers, worked through the terms of the agreement and how it would work. They also agreed that if for some reason Jane's approval was revoked then Peter would have the option to take over the mortgage and pay Jane out the same amount, as a backup.

They went through and listed all of the other items, such as who would keep what car and the furniture.

Jane's lawyer offered to write up the document and would collaborate with Peter's lawyer to finalise.

Once this was done, Peter and Jane signed off on the documents and they were filed in court. Both parties were extremely happy with the process; there were certainly some times when it was difficult to talk and discuss issues, but with the help and guidance of their two lawyers it kept the process on track and was sorted within just eight weeks.

The key in using the collaborative method is choosing the right lawyer, one that is trained in collaborative methods, and choosing two lawyers that can work well together. If you can achieve this then it will give you a huge head start to a calm settlement. I give my clients suggestions of other lawyers I work with and who I know are well trained and likeminded.

This option is a little more expensive than couples 2, 4 and 5, as there was the cost of the two lawyers, but it is a lot less than the court option which involves two lawyers, two barristers and experts in court. In my opinion it most certainly ticks all the boxes for kind, calm and peaceful. It is also a relatively quick option and results in a very positive relationship moving forward.

Court: the last option

I am choosing not to go into depth about this option in my book. The reason for this is that it is not what I call peaceful. I can honestly say that in my experience I have never had a matter in court that I could class as peaceful and therefore it should not form part of this book.

Sadly, Trish and Marcus ended up in this process; the reason for this, in my opinion, is that they started out all wrong.

Couple 1: Trish and Marcus

Ultimately, their matter went to court. They couldn't stop fighting. The hearing was two-and-a-half years after they originally filed the application. They both hired barristers and the hearing took five days, and they were both required to spend a whole day in the witness box being questioned on their contributions to the relationship. They also had to call an expert with regard to the value of the farm. In the end they received a judgement that specified the sum that Marcus had to pay Trish out.

Neither were really happy with the outcome.

Trish spent a little over $38,000 in legal fees and Marcus spent a lot more, having engaged a much more expensive lawyer at $65,000. In total they spent over $103,000 in fees and it took three years overall to get their result.

Trish and Marcus had no relationship by the end of it all. They shared the kids on a week about arrangement and the kids were swapped over at school so that they didn't have to see each other. They still from time to time sent each other a nasty text about money or something to do with the kids, but were never pleasant or kind to each other.

Although this avenue, in my experience, is the longest, most expensive, and has the worst outcome, it is still often chosen by couples. Looking back to their story it is clear to see exactly where things went wrong. Neither party is to blame, as both behaved badly, but if you look at their initial reactions, if they had thought things through carefully, sought some advice first and acted in a calm manner, perhaps their path would have been different. Rash and unplanned decisions, in my opinion, often turn out badly.

Wrapping it up

I am so hopeful by this stage that you will have an agreement. If you have mediated or worked through this collaboratively, still go back to chapter 6 and review your options for writing up the agreement. Get that agreement finalised so that you can move forward.

Conclusion

The writing of this book has taken me on a wonderful and inspiring personal journey. It has given me so much clarity, a clear perspective and guide on how my clients can help themselves. It has strengthened my view that I and other practitioners can do so much more for our clients; we can guide you in the right direction while following our own morals and values.

What I hope is very clear by now to you is that there are so many choices to be made along the journey of separation. That each choice can lead you along a very different path. That your own values, attitude and behaviour are primarily responsible for what path you do choose.

Rather than looking at your separation as being a legal problem to solve, we all really need to see it as a personal problem that you can have great control and power over. You are the author of your story.

Imagine a world where the majority of separated couples created their own solutions to separation and the minority were the ones in court. That is what I am fighting for. My ultimate dream, the reason I do this work, is so that couples can actually learn how to create a clear and peaceful path to separation. I want to educate as many people as possible, as many practitioners who are willing to learn, that there is nothing wrong with being a kind person or a kind lawyer, that there is often a people solution that is better than a legal solution; you just need to know how to find it.

I love being a kind lawyer and a mediator and truly enjoy working with couples. Whether it be my mediation process, working collaboratively or just teaching and guiding my clients to peaceful pathways, my work is rewarding for both myself and the couples that I lead.

At any stage of a separation you can come back to this book, come back to the ideas and theory, the process, and you can explain or give a copy to a friend, family member, colleague or other person you encounter that is going through this very difficult stage.

The more couples out there that fight for peace, that know that there is more to their separation than just the legal process and technicalities, that see kindness as a virtue and not a weakness, then the less fighting, money wasted, negativity and stress we will see.

Whether it be that you do it alone, or you can choose to engage a kind lawyer or mediator to assist you in mediation or collaborative work, may your fight always be for peace and kindness.

Work with Kirsty

Flourish Family Law was founded by Kirsty with the intention that couples could be educated and guided on what out-of-court solutions were available to them to solve their family law issues.

Flourish uses a kind and calm approach to all solutions, and combines the methods of negotiation, mediation, collaborative practice, as well as education and coaching on these techniques with the aim that you will save time and money in any family law dispute, and more importantly create a solution that is peaceful and calm.

All of Kirsty's work is aimed to help individuals, couples and families through this difficult time in the kindest and calmest way possible.

If you want to know more about Kirsty or how you can work with Kirsty to achieve these results, go to **flourishfamilylaw.com.au** or email her on **kirsty@flourishfamilylaw.com.au**.

Kirsty utilises her 18 years of knowledge as a Family Lawyer and her experience as an Accredited Mediator to assist her clients. The services she provides include:

Standard Mediation

Face-to-Face or online mediation services. Kirsty's style as a mediator is to get to know her clients, their needs and issues, in order to make the process feel very personal and the couples well supported. She focuses on teaching and guiding clients to prepare as much as possible themselves and to focus on behaviour, values and making good choices. Her role as a mediator helps clients by facilitating the process and assisting them with reaching agreements.

Collaborative Mediation

Face-to-face and online collaborative meetings. As discussed and taught in her book, Kirsty utilises other professionals such as accountants, financial planners and counsellors where needed. She has a unique staged system that allows couples to carefully and calmly navigate the process.

Settlement Negotiations

Kirsty, practising as a kind lawyer, has developed her own calming and kind style in negotiation, and prides herself on being able to negotiate your settlement, whether it be with your ex-spouse or their lawyer, so that you feel proud of your behaviour and choices at the end of the process.

Collaborative Practice

You can choose to engage Kirsty to assist you as your lawyer in the collaborative process, which involves the two parties and their lawyers working as a team to create your settlement solutions. Again, Kirsty utilises and has other experts ready to assist and join the team where necessary.

Settlement Agreements

If you have reached your own agreement, whether it be on your own, using Kirsty's Peaceful Pathway method, or with an independent mediator, she can also assist you by preparing your Settlement Agreement in a quick and amicable fashion.

Peaceful Pathways

- *Online and Downloadable Workbook:* You can slowly work your way through Kirsty's 6-step process and use her tips, tools and worksheets to get results.
- *Online Program:* An online, self-paced, do-it-yourself program specifically designed for amicable couples. This includes a copy of her book, the workbook and one hour of coaching directly with Kirsty.
- *Coaching Program:* An online or in-person, self-paced program. This includes a copy of her book, the workbook and six hours of coaching directly with Kirsty for each stage of the Peaceful Pathway process.

To find out more go to:
flourishfamilylaw.com.au/resources